When Someone Dies

The Practical Guide to the Logistics of Death

Scott Taylor Smith

with Michael Castleman

SCRIBNER

New York   London   Toronto   Sydney   New Delhi

Scribner
A Division of Simon & Schuster, Inc.
1230 Avenue of the Americas
New York, NY 10020

Copyright © 2013 by Scott Smith

First Scribner trade paperback edition March 2013

SCRIBNER and design are registered trademarks of The Gale Group, Inc.,
used under license by Simon & Schuster, Inc., the publisher of this work.

For information about special discounts for bulk purchases, please contact Simon &
Schuster Special Sales at 1-866-506-1949 or business@simonandschuster.com.

The Simon & Schuster Speakers Bureau can bring authors to your live event. For
more information or to book an event, contact the Simon & Schuster Speakers
Bureau at 1-866-248-3049 or visit our website at www.simonspeakers.com.

Designed by Katy Riegel

Manufactured in the United States of America

3 5 7 9 10 8 6 4 2

Library of Congress Control Number: 2012028413

ISBN 978-1-4767-0021-2
ISBN 978-1-4767-0024-3 (ebook)

Legal Disclaimer

Laws dealing with death and inheritance are complex and vary considerably by state and nation. While we have done everything possible to be accurate, including consulting with top estate attorneys, this book is no substitute for professional legal advice. For the laws in your particular location, we urge you to consult an attorney.

Contents

Contents

Chapter 1

As Death Approaches

Contents

Chapter 2
Immediately after the Death

Chapter 3

The Days after the Death: Nonfinancial Issues

Chapter 4

The Days and Weeks after the Death: Financial Issues

Contents

Chapter 5
The Year after the Death

Chapter 6
You're Done; Now Make Things Easy for Your Survivors

Appendix:
Sample Legal Forms and a Model Obituary

Contents

Acknowledgments

The authors are deeply indebted to James Mitchell, a partner in the San Francisco law firm Coblentz, Patch, Duffy & Bass, who graciously provided insights from the perspective of an estates and trust lawyer. The laws regarding settlement of estates are complex and they vary greatly from state to state. The authors have done their best to provide an accurate, albeit simple, summary of core principles and rules, but it is essential that you contact a qualified estates and trust lawyer when making any decision about an estate. This book is not and should not be regarded as legal advice by Mr. Mitchell or the authors.

In addition, deepest thanks to our agent, Amy Rennert of the Amy Rennert Agency, Tiburon, California, and to the agency's Robyn Russell and Louise Kollenbaum. Thanks also to our editor at Scribner, Shannon Welch. Finally, thank you to our publicist, Sophie Vershbow.

Scott Smith thanks Marcelo and his family and friends.

Michael Castleman thanks his wife, Anne Simons; his children, Maya, Jeff, and Kristen; and his estate attorney, David Miller.

Quick Reference Guide

Some death-related tasks are time-sensitive. For example, advance directives are very important as death approaches, but once the person has died, they no longer matter. Other tasks—for example, the funeral—have longer trajectories. They involve tasks that may begin before the death and extend months or even years after it. The Quick Reference Guide directs you to all the information about key subjects throughout the book so that you can make good decisions in an efficient and timely fashion.

The Funeral

Obtaining Money for the Funeral

In Chapter 2:

Pay the Mortuary (46).

In Chapter 4:

Pay Funeral Expenses (64).

If the Person Was Employed, Collect Final Wages and Other Payments (68).

Collect the Social Security Death Benefit (69).

Investigate Social Security Survivor Benefits (70).

Investigate Veterans Administration and Other Federal Government Benefits (72).

Find the Person's Assets (78).

Paying the Person's Bills

In Chapter 2:

Pay the Mortuary (46).

In Chapter 4:

Pay Funeral Expenses (64).

If the Person Was Employed, Collect Final Wages and Other Payments (68).

Collect the Social Security Death Benefit (69).

Investigate Social Security Survivor Benefits (70).

Investigate Veterans Administration and Other Federal Government Benefits (72).

No Probate? Or Probate? And If So, Which Type?

Distributing the Estate's Assets

When Someone Dies

Introduction

If you're reading this book, someone you love has just died. We feel your pain. As you'll read, I recently lost a loved one, and I've endured the grief that now consumes you. My heart breaks for you.

Grieving is a uniquely individual process. Don't let anyone tell you what's supposedly "normal" or the "best" way to grieve.

Most people find that grief is like swimming in the ocean. It comes in waves. One minute you feel fine, then the next you dissolve in tears. Ride the waves and try not to resist them. If you resist, just as if you swim against the current in the ocean, you might drown.

We urge you to explore all the emotions your grief raises—including relief, if that applies. We urge you to obtain all the emotional support you need—from friends, family, clergy, and perhaps a grief counselor and/or support group. We also urge you to read some of the many books on grieving. Our favorite is quite brief (only ninety pages) but remarkably profound—*A Grief Observed* by C. S. Lewis.

But this is *not* a book about grief or grieving. Instead, this is a succinct, step-by-step guide to all the practical things *you must do* after someone dies to settle the person's affairs as quickly and cost-effectively as possible. If you follow our advice, your life will be easier, the costs associated with the death will be much lower, and you'll find that you and other grieving family members and friends will get along much better.

Of course, no one enjoys dealing with bureaucracies—funeral homes, banks, the Internal Revenue Service (IRS), Social Security, and so on. And it's particularly alienating to have to do it *now*. But some decisions can't wait, and if you're the one dealing with the practicalities—the executor of the decedent's estate—this book should lighten your burden.

How long does it take to deal with the practical details of death? Expect to spend a considerable amount of time and energy during the first thirty days and more over the next six months to a year. The process is challenging and potentially infuriating, but it's important—and *absolutely necessary*. If you're organized, if you follow the path we provide, it shouldn't drive you crazy. It's also part of the grieving process, an integral part of saying goodbye, tying up loose ends, and making peace with your loss.

I stumbled on the need for this book when my mother died in 2009. I'm an attorney. I'd dealt professionally with wills, trusts, and estates, and I knew my mother's affairs were in reasonably good order. I thought—naïvely, it turned out—that dealing with the practical issues surrounding her death would take only a few days. I was so wrong. It took two years, and I made several costly mistakes because I didn't have a guide like this one. I thought no one should have to go through what I endured—and if you follow the step-by-step program we've outlined, you won't.

My Mother's Death

I want to share some details of my mother's death because they provide a context for this book. When someone dies, people imagine the family coming together and drawing closer to say goodbye. But my family was torn apart. We fought and for a while became emotionally distant. All of the "issues" you've had with your loved one, siblings, and other relatives come to the fore, and like my sisters and me, you may revert to the family dynamics you experienced as children . . . even if you don't want to.

My mother was eighty-five, healthy, and living independently in Santa Rosa, California, when she tripped and fell in a parking lot near her home, smashing her head on the pavement. My sister Tory was with her and immediately called 911. The paramedic said she was bleeding into her brain. The prognosis was grim.

Tory called me from the ambulance. I was at work in San Francisco, sixty miles to the south. My presence was especially urgent because I held my mother's medical power of attorney (see page 135). I was the one who would have the final say on her medical decisions. I grabbed the file marked "Mom" and jumped into my car.

The emergency room doctor confirmed the paramedic's diagnosis, bleeding into the brain. He determined that she had only a few hours to live.

"If she were young," he explained, "we'd open her skull and drain the blood. We could do that for your mother, but at her age, the procedure could easily kill her. What do you want to do?"

I'd helped my mother draft a living will. In it, she'd included a do-not-resuscitate order (DNR), in which she'd stated unequivocally that she wanted no extraordinary measures taken to prolong her life. I informed the doctor, who said, "Fine."

But just then, my mother suddenly regained consciousness and seemed remarkably lucid. (I learned later that among those with brain trauma, this happens fairly frequently.) The doctor spoke to Mom, explaining the situation, and asked her if she wanted surgery or no treatment.

Without hesitation, she replied, "Open me up! I don't want to die!" Then she slipped out of consciousness into a coma-like sleep.

I was aghast. She'd overruled her living will—but was she competent to make the decision? My other sisters, Kim and Terry, arrived, and the four of us had no idea what to do.

Someone called the hospital's medical ethicist—the patient ombudsman—who met us in the emergency room. She asked the doctor, "If you operate, what are her chances of returning to her previous quality of life?"

The doctor replied, "Near zero." My siblings and I split two to two. One sister and I wanted to follow the living will's instructions. The other two wanted surgery. But I held the power of attorney, so ultimately it was my decision. I decided against surgery, reminding everyone that Mom had emphatically said "no extraordinary measures." That did not sit well with the two opposing sisters.

I felt awful. Our mother was critically injured and dying. I'd hoped the four of us would come to a consensus—but here we were seriously divided.

Then things got worse. Since I'd decided against surgery, the issue became how to make Mom comfortable. The doctor wanted to prescribe large doses of morphine because brain injuries like my mother's cause excruciating pain. But Mom was drifting in and out of consciousness, and two sisters argued that morphine would crush her remaining lucidity. "If she can talk," they said, "I want to talk to her."

I saw their point, but the doctor said, "If this were my mother, I'd give morphine. I wouldn't want her in pain."

I said, "Okay, morphine." My sisters became furious and didn't speak to me for several days.

With the doctors united in the opinion that nothing could be done to save my mother, they could not keep her in the hospital and sent her to hospice care at a skilled nursing facility. The nurses there gave her regular high doses of morphine. But one sister felt an overpowering need to talk to Mom. She hated seeing her "drugged" and tried to interfere with the nurses, at one point even ordering them to stop administering the morphine.

When I heard about it, I exploded. "This is cruel," I screamed, but my sister felt frantic—we all did—and she couldn't hear me. We were at each other's throats, and worse, we were hurting our mother, whom we all dearly loved.

I called the neurosurgeon, who graciously offered to stop by the facility. He sat the four of us down and said, "Your mother is going to die—and very soon. There's nothing medicine can do to change that. Recovery is impossible. She's virtually brain-dead right now. If you want her comfortable, you must give morphine."

At that point, everyone accepted the inevitable.

We kept looking at Mom, expecting every breath to be her last. But somehow she survived for ten more very sad, tension-filled days. The only thing that kept us halfway sane was the steady stream of visitors who cycled through Mom's care unit. She had lots of friends. She'd had a long career as a psychotherapist, and she'd mentored many younger therapists, dozens of whom visited. No one came empty-handed. We had more food and flowers than we knew what to do with. Finally, Mom died.

We were raised high Episcopal, but I'd been attending a Catholic church with my spouse. Meanwhile, one sister had practiced Buddhism for many years, and she arranged for Buddhist death-related ceremonies. They were compassionate, extraordinary rituals, but they included leaving the remains in the home for seven days to insure safe passage of the soul to heaven. To my way of thinking, having Mom lie dead in her home for seven days was simply wrong—impractical and unhealthy, given the speed of postmortem decomposition. But to my sister, the ritual was a moral imperative. She believed deeply that seven days of rest were *essential* for the safe passage of Mom's soul to heaven. What if she were right and I was wrong?

After much discussion, we agreed on two days with Mom's body packed in dry ice. Our compromise worked. Many people came to the house and sat with Mom and said goodbye. It turned out to be a beautiful passage for Mom, for our family, and for her close friends.

When Mom died, I thought, naïvely, that her death would bring closure. Actually, it brought the flood of responsibilities and critical decisions that led to this book.

I felt so disoriented. One day, Mom was fine, and then, suddenly, she'd sustained a fatal brain injury. I couldn't think straight. Meanwhile, I was her executor, and people started asking all sorts of questions: Was she an organ donor? How would you like to dispose of her body? Which funeral home? Burial or cremation? What kind of service?

Mom had answered many of these questions in her living will and other documents. I'd helped prepare them, but at the crucial moment when this information became necessary, I was lost in grief and couldn't find it. Fortunately, I recalled the name of her attorney, and he had copies.

The moment someone dies, it suddenly feels like *everyone* wants you to decide something, and they're big decisions. For example:

- Hospitals give you only a few hours to deal with organ donation, and less than twenty-four hours to dispose of the body.
- Which mortuary? Hospitals want the body removed as quickly as possible.
- How do you move a body? Only a licensed mortuary, a hospital, or law enforcement can legally move a body. The mortuary can charge a surprisingly large amount.

- Cremation? Or burial? Closed casket? Or open? The funeral home needs to know very quickly.
- Doctors and hospitals don't inform Social Security about deaths. You have to—and if you don't, the government can fine you. Who knew?
- If you tell the bank about the death the *right* way, you can close the accounts, withdrawing assets and emptying any safe-deposit boxes. But if you tell the bank the *wrong* way, all funds are likely to be frozen for months. I did it the wrong way and gnashed my teeth.
- Everyone you deal with demands a death certificate, and many families run out of copies, which becomes a costly, time-consuming hassle. (Shortly after Mom died, a friend's father passed away. I called him and said, "I'm so sorry." Then I implored, "Order twenty-five death certificates right now. Trust me, you won't regret it." He later said this was the single best piece of advice he received.)
- Who pays for the funeral home? They don't take the body until someone commits to paying for the funeral.
- You have to write the obituary yourself and pay the newspaper by the word to publish it.

I had to learn all this—and much more—the hard way. Now you don't have to.

Who Should Read This Book

When Someone Dies is for everyone who finds themselves contending with the logistics and practicalities of closing out a loved one's earthly presence. In particular, we've written this book with executors (or trustees) in mind. These are the people (usually) named by the decedent while still living to deal with the aftermath of the death and the myriad tasks and decisions that follow from it. (We explain the terms "executor," "trustee," and "power of attorney" in the following pages.) When we say "you," we mean the executor or trustee, though you may choose to delegate some of the responsibilities we discuss. That's fine; however, if you're the executor, you should understand that you and only you are legally responsible for the timely settling of the person's estate, including payment of all debts and taxes due, distribution of all net assets, termination of Social Security and other benefits that end at death, and many other tedious chores. This involves real work, time, and effort, which is why executors are paid a fee.

By law in most states, the executor or trustee is entitled (and sometimes required) to take a fee, typically 2 percent of the value of the estate. I was my mother's trustee, but some family members objected to my taking the fee. Fortunately, I did not need the money, so I offered to donate my fee to Mom's favorite charity. That made everyone happy.

If the person did not name an executor, the law requires that someone step into that role—first the spouse, and if there is no spouse, then the children, typically in descending age order.

Answers to Key Questions

This book provides clear, concise answers to the key questions that arise when someone dies, among them:

- Who has the authority to act on behalf of the decedent?
- How do I get access to the person's financial assets—bank accounts, investments, and so on?
- Do I—or does anyone—have to pay the person's debts, for example, the mortgage and credit card debts?
- How do we decide who gets to live in the house? Who pays the mortgage?
- How do I transfer ownership of the house? The car? Other assets?

How to Use This Book

We've organized this guide temporally to cover what you need to know and do as the death becomes imminent, the immediate aftermath of the death, the few days to a week or so after, several weeks to several months after, and months to a year or so after. We've arranged the book this way because that's how the responsibilities confront you, the executor: first this list of tasks, then the next list. We've also provided checklists at the beginning of each chapter to provide an overview and to help you get organized.

In addition, we've provided a Quick Reference Guide to key elements of the process. For example, we discuss the tasks related to the funeral and any memorial tasks in Chapters 1, 2, 3, and 5. If you'd like to focus on the funeral-memorial, the Quick Reference Guide can point you to all the information, wherever it may be.

We've designed the Table of Contents and Index to provide quick, easy access to whatever interests you. Finally, in the Appendices we have provided everything from an Advanced Health Care Directive to a Model Obituary for your reference. You probably won't need to reference every single one of these documents, but it's handy to have them in one place if you do. More forms are available on our Web site, WhenSomeoneDies. net.

If you have a question not answered in the text, please visit our Web site to ask your question. We'll reply as soon as possible.

1

As Death Approaches

❑ Who's in charge before the death?

❑ Does the person have an advance health care directive (living will)?

❑ Does the person have a durable power of attorney for health care?

❑ If the person prepared an advance directive and a durable power of attorney for health care, find those documents.

❑ Attend to your own well-being.

❏ Attend to the person's comfort.

❏ Start contacting family and friends.

❏ Who's in charge after the death?

❏ Has the person specified an executor?

❏ The executor must register with the Internal Revenue Service. (The estate may also need an employer identification number—see Chapter 4.)

❏ Avoid theft.

❏ Start thinking about the funeral.

❏ Shop for a mortuary.

❏ Will an autopsy be necessary?

❏ Start thinking about body preparation: embalming? No embalming? Or "green"?

❏ Consider thanking end-of-life caregivers.

Note: This chapter assumes that the death occurs with family gathered by the bedside as the person's life slips away. If the death occurs suddenly and without warning (an accident, suicide, sudden illness, etc.), many of these tasks become moot, for example, attending to the person's comfort and acting on advance directives. But many other tasks must still be accomplished, notably, shopping for a mortuary and planning the funeral. See pages 41–42 for a discussion about what to do if the death involved a crime or was caused by a third party, such as in a car accident.

Who's in Charge before the Death?

If the person dying is a mentally competent adult, that person has the legal authority to make all decisions about his or her own life, including decisions regarding medical care. But when someone is incapacitated, families often squabble over who has the right to make decisions. For minor children, the parents make the decisions. But what about making decisions for an adult?

Many people anticipate this possibility and while they are of sound mind, appoint someone as their "agent" by naming them in a document called a "durable power of attorney" (for a sample, see the Appendix). A power of attorney may be limited to health care decisions (advance medical directive), it may focus on financial matters, or it may deal with both. If the person has signed a durable power of attorney, read it carefully to make sure you actually have the specific power you want to exercise.

If the person's mental competence is questionable—drifting in and out of consciousness or seeming conscious but saying things out of character or that contradict a living will—consult a medical ethicist. Hospitals and hospices usually have a patient ombudsman or hospital ethicist on call.

If the dying person is unconscious or is mentally incompetent because of dementia or some other brain injury, the person in charge is the one named in a durable power of attorney for health care.

If there is no durable power of attorney for health care, then by law, the decision maker is the spouse. If there is no spouse, then it's the parents of the child or the adult children of the parent—either the only child present or, if several are, then often in descending age order. If there are no spouse and no kids, then a sibling has the power. And if there are no relatives, then the power often resides with the government.

Does the Person Have an Advance Health Care Directive (Living Will)?

Ideally, the person completed an advance directive (living will) that specifies instructions for end-of-life medical care. Typically, an advance directive says: "I do not want any extraordinary procedures used to prolong my life. I do not want to be kept alive in a vegetative state." In other words, an advance directive says: "When I'm ready to go, let me go." But a living will may specify other choices, for example, *desiring* all life-prolonging procedures, no matter how invasive or traumatic.

Advance directives appoint a "health care agent" who becomes responsible for making sure that health care providers follow the person's instructions. Laws vary from state to state, but advance directives without a power of attorney are typically not legally binding on the family and on medical personnel. To make them binding, the person needs a durable power of attorney for health care. Most states have combined these documents into one form (see the Appendix for a sample California form).

Does the Person Have a Durable Power of Attorney for Health Care?

This document names a person and gives that person the legal authority—the power of attorney—to enforce the person's advance directive for end-of-life care on the family and on medical personnel who might otherwise not follow the person's wishes.

If you're that person, you may have to contend with family and close friends who disagree with your decisions. That happened to me; as I explain in the Introduction, one of my sisters became furious with the decision I took about our mother's care. For better or worse, that's the price of being the person's attorney of record for health care.

You may also have to contend with medical personnel disregarding the wishes of the person who holds the durable power of attorney. Some doctors think it's their right to use extraordinary measures even if the dying person doesn't want them and even if the person holding the durable power of attorney says, "Stop! Don't do that."

If medical personnel ignore you, first, present a united front. Gather family and friends and start screaming if you have to—the more people, the better. If that doesn't work, contact a hospital administrator and the hospital's patient ombudsman. Tell them that the doctor in question is breaking the law by ignoring an advance directive backed up by a durable power of attorney, which opens the hospital to legal liability. And if that doesn't work, call the police. A physician who acts contrary to an advance directive backed up by a durable power of attorney is committing assault and battery and is subject to arrest.

Recently, many states have adopted a form called the Physician's Orders for Life-Sustaining Treatment (POLST; see Appendix for a sample). It's signed by both the patient and the doctor while the patient is still healthy to demonstrate that the doctor is aware of the patient's wishes and agrees to comply with the patient's end-of-life medical decisions. It does not replace the advance medical directive and power of attorney, but it supplements them.

If the Person Prepared an Advance Directive and a Durable Power of Attorney for Health Care, Find Those Documents

While in the prime of life, many people—but by no means all—hire an estate lawyer to draw up these documents and a will. If your loved one dies and you haven't been made privy to these documents, check with the lawyer, who will have kept copies of them.

If you don't know the name of the lawyer in question, you may wish to check with other attorneys your loved one dealt with. For example, the lawyers who handled a divorce or a sale of the house probably won't have the person's will, but it's possible that they might or they might know the identity of the estate-planning lawyer, so check with every attorney you know the person has ever used.

If you don't even know whether the person had these documents drafted, then you must look for them. Start with the person's desk and file cabinet. Often these documents are kept in a loose-leaf binder. If you can't find them around the house, ask relatives and the person's close friends. If you have access to the person's computer, look there. But the most likely place is a safe-deposit box at a bank. Most banks will allow you immediate but limited access to another person's safe-deposit box if you have the key and/or a death certificate; you will be allowed to inventory items and make copies of documents. Before you can remove items of value, the bank typically requires proof that you are the executor or are otherwise authorized to remove the material.

If you find the papers, follow the person's instructions. If not, then the decision-making authority rests first with the spouse; second, the children; and third, other relatives or close friends. Executors are not involved in this, except to the extent that they are blood relatives. The executor's job begins *after* the death.

Written instructions are especially important for those in gay, lesbian, or nontraditional relationships. Without them, gay, lesbian, and nontraditional significant others may not have the legal authority to make *any* decisions.

Everyone should have a written will, advance directive, and medical power of attorney. You can find more on this in Chapter 6.

What Happens When Family Members Disagree about Medical Intervention?

Doctors and nurses are usually sensitive and caring. If it's clear that the family has reached a consensus about stopping life support, the staff will stop it—assuming that they are convinced that the family has come to an agreement. If you reach a consensus, make sure the person's doctors and nurses know.

But things get murky when the hospital staff perceives family disagreement. For example, say Dad died years ago, and Mom didn't remarry, so there's no spouse to make end-of-life care decisions, and the person's children (and possibly other relatives) are squabbling about what to do.

All the siblings and the other relatives have influence, but the person in charge is the one named in the dying person's durable power of attorney for health care. That person has *all* legal authority. If three siblings, two cousins, and an aunt and uncle all want surgery, while the person named in the power of attorney wants hospice care, the person goes to hospice.

If there is no power of attorney, most states provide that the spouse (or the parents in the absence of a spouse) has the authority to decide and, in some cases, siblings. In the absence of such a provision, the executor or family needs to go to court to be appointed as legal guardian and decision-maker.

Attend to Your Own Well-Being

On airplanes you're told, "If you are traveling with anyone who needs assistance, put *your* oxygen mask on first, and then help those traveling with you." Why? Because you can't help anyone if you're gasping for air. You have to take care of yourself first.

Waiting for the death of someone you love is traumatic. Be kind to yourself. You can't be there for anyone else if you're gasping for air. Do things that help you manage your stress, for example, meditation or yoga. Many people find that exercise helps; take walks around the hospital. If music calms you, use an iPod or sing and play for the person—studies show that even people in comas hear what goes on around them. There's no need for the whole family to stay at the bedside all the time, so take turns to stay or take a break. Get some sleep. As the end approaches, those who are not by the bed can be called back by phone when necessary.

Attend to the Person's Comfort

You're probably familiar with the term "death rattle," the sound that dying people make as their lives end. It's not a rattle exactly, more like a wheezy, raspy gasping. It happens because as death approaches, the lungs fill with fluid and breathing becomes labored—and noisy.

Sometimes, the dying person spews phlegm. It's not a pretty sight, and it usually frightens those gathered around the bedside. It's messy, and the person dying looks to be in distress. If the death takes place in a hospital or skilled nursing facility, nurses stop by periodically with a device that painlessly sucks out excess fluid and mucus, minimizing the sound and any spewing. But if the death takes place somewhere else, you may hear and see more than you want to.

As it becomes clear that the person is very near death, the main issue is the person's comfort. Most hospitals, hospices, and nursing homes are generous with morphine, the world's best pain reliever. Morphine is also addictive, but when people are dying, that doesn't matter. What matters is their comfort, and no drug on earth is as effective at comforting the dying as morphine. Welcome its use.

Sometimes the dying person lingers in life longer than anticipated and appears uncomfortable or agitated despite standard doses of morphine. When this happens, family and friends typically feel helpless and often frantic. In the past, doctors often took matters into their own hands and "helped" their patients die. Because of the threat of malpractice claims, today doctors are much more reluctant to do this. Today, people in hospice often provide the family with the means to hasten the end. For example, a hospice nurse may appear with a handful of pills or syringe, saying, "This is a high dose of morphine. I can't give it because it would accelerate death, which is illegal. You shouldn't give it either." Then the nurse places the pills or syringe on a bedside table and leaves the room. You're then free to let your conscience be your guide.

But be careful. In most states, it's illegal to hasten death. If everyone at the bedside agrees that the pills or shot should be given, you may do so, though you risk someone regretting the decision and pointing an accusing finger: "He killed Mom!" You know your family. Discuss what you'd like to do at this very difficult moment.

As death approaches, especially when people are taking high doses of morphine, they may talk and hallucinate. Sometimes it's beautifully spiritual. They may see a bright light or a vision of heaven. On the other hand, it may be the opposite. Sometimes dying people say awful things: "I never loved you." They don't mean it; it's the drugs talking.

Start Contacting Family and Friends

At this stage you're under no obligation to contact everyone, just those who would want to be there for the person's final moments—immediate family and the person's closest friends. However, we recommend erring on the side of contacting more than just close family and friends. Everyone who knows the person cares, wants to know what's happening, and wants to offer help. Friends and acquaintances will appreciate the chance to know what's happening and if possible to help; and in the long run, you will appreciate that you let them in.

There are some fantastic information-sharing Web sites for just this purpose, such as Caring.com. You can upload e-mail addresses, and it's very easy to broadcast updates to those on the list. These sites also include coordination functions so you can schedule visits efficiently.

Who's in Charge after the Death?

In most states, upon death all powers of attorney automatically expire, and the person named in any power-of-attorney document is no longer in charge. After the death, the person in charge is the executor (or trustee) of the estate.

Has the Person Specified an Executor?

The executor is the administrator of the decedent's estate. How do you learn who that is? Typically, the will names the executor. Most wills also designate "successor" executors if the first one dies or for any reason can't fulfill the executor's responsibilities or does not want to. You're free to decline the executor role. If the will does not name a successor executor, in most states the named executor may recommend someone for the job. Any successor who has not been named would typically require court approval.

Executors should read this book very carefully because they are responsible for all the tasks we discuss: paying the person's debts and taxes, distributing the person's assets, dealing with probate (if necessary), and settling the person's affairs. If the person has taken the steps we recommend in Chapter 6, the executor's job can be fairly straightforward and only moderately time-consuming. But if the person hasn't taken those steps or has vast wealth or a complex family situation (for example, five children by three husbands), then the executor's job becomes complicated, convoluted, and *very* time-consuming.

If the person has not specified an executor, or if the family and close friends don't know who the executor is, then someone has to petition the probate court for the job. Contact a lawyer. Once the court appoints the volunteer, that person becomes the executor.

The Executor Must Register with the Internal Revenue Service

As the saying goes, "Nothing is certain except death and taxes." While some debts can go unpaid (see Chapter 4), the executor must pay any taxes the person or the estate owes.

Executors handle other people's money, meaning that they act in "a fiduciary capacity." The law requires anyone in a fiduciary role to file Internal Revenue Service (IRS) form 56, "Notice Concerning Fiduciary Relationship." This form can be obtained at any IRS office or online from the IRS Web site at http://www.irs.gov/pub/irs-pdf/f56.pdf.

Avoid Theft

We hate to say it, but when someone dies, the valuables they carry—rings, watches, and so on—have a way of disappearing somewhere between the scene of the death and the funeral. Possible culprits include hospital and mortuary personnel and friends and relatives.

Don't take chances. If you have not already done so, remove the person's rings, necklaces, watch, wallet or purse, and other valuables immediately after the death.

Again, we hate to say it, but neighbors, friends, and relatives may enter the home to steal the person's belongings (or take them in the belief they have a right to them). You may not know who has keys to the person's home. As quickly as possible after the death, call a locksmith and have the locks changed. Post a note on the door announcing what you've done, and invite anyone who needs access—cleaning people, the gardener, and so on—to contact you. Provide your phone number and e-mail address.

Start Thinking about the Funeral

It may seem premature, even heartless, to think about the funeral while the person is still alive. But some religions—for example, Judaism—require burial as quickly as possible after death. Others allow more flexibility in the timing of funerals. Many religious traditions also call for sacraments and other formal practices in the hours before death, so it's a good idea to consult with an appropriate member of the clergy early on. Regardless of the person's religion, a clergy member will ensure that you observe the rituals that the person would have wanted both before and after they pass.

Shop for a Mortuary

Many funeral homes are good, honest businesses. They provide an invaluable service. However, as with any business, their aim is profitability, and their goal is to maximize what you spend in your hours of grief and emotional disarray. And the unscrupulous ones are very good at using your emotional distress to pick your pocket. Before you decide on a mortuary, we urge you in the strongest possible terms to compile a list of everything you want—transportation of the remains, embalming or not, cremation, burial, and so on—and then contact two or three mortuaries and compare their prices *before* you release the remains to any of them. Of course, when someone dies, the last thing you want to do is to go shopping. But if you don't shop, you're much more likely to be scammed, possibly for thousands of dollars.

Which mortuaries should you call? Some have religious affiliations that you might embrace or want to avoid, but beyond that, it doesn't really matter. Mortuaries are like car dealers— all pretty much the same. Shop for convenience and, above all, price. Ask your friends and relatives for a recommendation and ask how much they paid. Also check the Internet for social commentary. Once people have survived a funeral, they tend to like to talk about it, so don't be afraid to ask people about their experiences.

First shop for the big-ticket item, the casket. Caskets start at a few hundred dollars for a plain plywood or pine box and go up to tens of thousands of dollars for tropical woods, gold fittings, and silk lining. Typically, the funeral director will show you caskets in five price ranges. Marketing studies show very clearly that given five choices with ascending prices, very few naïve buyers—and most funeral shoppers are naïve—opt for the cheapest or most expensive choices. The vast majority select the middle option or the one right above it in price. Those two choices are substantially more expensive than the two cheapest options.

You don't have to buy a casket. If you're so inclined, you can build your own or commission one and deliver it to the mortuary. Select the casket that suits your family and your budget, but we urge you to remember that anything other than a metal casket will start to decompose immediately. A casket is a very temporary home; ashes to ashes, dust to dust.

If you balk at a pricey casket, expect the funeral director to attempt to shame you with maudlin appeals to the deceased's dignity: "*That* box? *Really*? It's your *mother*. . . ." It usually doesn't take much for a funeral director to push those who are newly bereaved (and not always entirely of sound mind at the time) to spend a great deal more than they'd planned. Buyer, beware! It's smart to bring a friend with you to negotiate. You need to remain strong and remember that the person who died has likely gone to heaven (or to a "better place" or wherever your religious beliefs tell you) and the casket likely does not hold the person's soul. And if you opt for an open casket, the funeral director will hit you up for all sorts of extra charges for hairdressing, makeup, shaving, a manicure and so on.

Mortuaries also charge a bundle for flowers. Consider providing your own. In fact, consider asking family and friends to bring flowers to the funeral. People want to do something to help—asking them to bring flowers will make them feel useful. They'll feel they've contributed, and you'll have a flower-filled funeral to show how beloved the person was, which might soothe your grief a bit.

Mortuaries also charge for every moment of transit: from the place of death to the mortuary, and to the burial site. They even charge for placing mementos in the casket: photos, a crucifix, a sports team hat. These charges really add up.

If you opt for cremation, funeral directors often try to sell you *two* items—a casket for the funeral and cremation and an urn for the ashes. They may imply that an urn is legally required for ashes. That's not true. You're free to take the ashes in any container you like, even a plastic bag. Always ask: Is this required by law? When put on the spot, most funeral directors tell the truth or close to it—at least in states with active departments of consumer affairs that send secret shoppers to businesses like funeral parlors and auto shops, places notorious for fraud.

We cremated my mother—without a casket. The funeral director was aghast and tried very hard to sell us a cherrywood casket for $7,800. We said no thanks. Then he tried to sell us an urn for her ashes. Urns start at a few hundred dollars and can go up to thousands. Again we declined. By law, the mortuary must supply a cardboard or wood container for you to carry the ashes away in. That's what we received—Mom's ashes in a cardboard box. I took them home and left the box on the mantel for a few months, then we distributed her ashes around the top of the hill on my property, a spot she adored. Both she and my stepfather have bronze plaques near the spot where we scattered her ashes.

A note on open-casket funerals. You must provide clothes to dress the body, and you'll probably pay a dressing charge. State laws usually do not require embalming for closed-casket services, but if the casket is open, you *must* embalm. If anyone touches a corpse that has not been embalmed, it might release nasty decomposition gases that smell awful. The body might even explode—yes, *explode*.

For more information on arranging a funeral, contact the mortuary trade organization, the International Cemetery, Cremation, and Funeral Association, at http://www.iccfa.com.

For more on your rights as a funeral consumer, visit the Federal Trade Commission at http://ftc.gov/bcp/menus/consumer/shop/funeral.shtm or the Funeral Consumer Guardian Society at http://www.funeralconsumer.org. The latter site can help you estimate costs.

Will an Autopsy Be Necessary?

An autopsy will probably not be necessary. Autopsies are required only if medical or law enforcement authorities suspect foul play or an infectious disease or other public health hazard. You can find more on autopsies in Chapter 2.

Start Thinking about Body Preparation:
Embalming? No Embalming? Or "Green"?

Mortuaries push embalming and often imply that it's legally required. In most states, embalming is optional; however, it may be required in warm climates because heat spurs decomposition.

Embalming fluid and other chemicals used in traditional burial preparation eventually become incorporated into the ground and may contaminate the soil and groundwater. "Green" burials, on the other hand, prepare the body without potentially polluting chemicals and contain the body in a cloth shroud or a biodegradable casket rather than metal.

Since the 1990s, green burials have become increasingly popular. Compared with traditional burials, they cause less ground and water contamination and have a smaller carbon footprint.

Some people believe that cremation is automatically green. It's green *only* if the remains are not embalmed.

Green body preparation is not available everywhere. If you're interested, ask when you shop for a mortuary, or visit the Green Burial Council at http://www.greenburialcouncil.org.

Consider Thanking End-of-Life Caregivers

It's amazing how quickly you can feel close to medical and/or hospice personnel who care for a loved one as death approaches. Many people use the word "saint." If you're moved by the care the person received, thank those who provided it. Many families use the obituary to acknowledge publicly a loved one's care providers. It's also a good idea to compile a list of caregivers' names, phone numbers, street addresses, and e-mail addresses. You may want to send thank-you notes, give gratuities, or make charitable donations in their honor. And if questions arise about the death (from insurers, the coroner, etc.), you'll know who to contact and how to find them.

To avoid the risk of impropriety many rest homes and hospices forbid the payment of gratuities. You should check to see what is allowed.

2

Immediately after the Death

CHECKLIST

❑ Contact family and friends.

❑ Identify important advisors—lawyers, accountants, and financial advisors.

❑ Welcome small gestures of support and comfort.

❑ Be prepared for insensitivity.

❑ Begin certifying the death.

❑ If the person is an organ donor or arranged for whole-body donation, follow through with those arrangements.

- ❑ Ask about an autopsy.

- ❑ Murder, accidents, and suicide.

- ❑ If the remains must be shipped elsewhere, arrange for shipping.

- ❑ Arrange care for the person's children, pets, and yard.

- ❑ File a change-of-address form with the Post Office.

- ❑ Obtain two to three dozen original copies of the death certificate.

- ❑ Pay the mortuary.

- ❑ Burial or cremation?

- ❑ For burials, purchase a grave site.

- ❑ To avoid theft during the funeral, arrange for someone to house-sit the person's home.

Note: If the person died suddenly, you must accomplish several of the tasks discussed in Chapter 1, notably, shopping for a mortuary and planning the funeral.

Contact Family and Friends

It's painful, sometimes tragic and horrible, but people want to know. Tell them as quickly as possible, and encourage them to spread the word. You might want to put someone in charge of informing everyone. That leaves you with more time to manage the dozens of other details.

When possible, announce the death to people face-to-face. It helps to hold each other and cry together. Quite often, however, face-to-face announcements are inconvenient or impossible. Advice columnists waste a good deal of ink on "appropriate" ways to inform people of painful events. We firmly believe that telling people simply and quickly by any means available is better than delaying or not telling them. Phone, e-mail, texting, Facebook, Twitter—whatever's handy, use it.

Tell everyone with any connection to the person. People want to know because they yearn to offer comfort and condolences. In addition, tell those connected to *you*. Death is a big deal. The people you know want to know and want to be there for you. Of course, it's time-consuming to field condolences from dozens of people and help them process their own shock and grief. But when faced with loss, emotional support really helps. We're a social species. We need contact with our fellow humans, especially when times get tough.

People also want to help by providing food or assistance with logistics—picking up people at airports, for example.

Identify Important Advisors—Lawyers, Accountants, and Financial Advisors

If the person who died had considerable assets—a home, stocks and bonds, a retirement account—the likelihood is that you will need support and advice from lawyers, accountants, and financial advisors. More likely than not, the person who died already has a good lawyer and other advisors looking out for him or her. It is essential that you locate these people and notify them of the death. They will be in the best position to help you figure out all of the financial issues like paying taxes, getting access to cash, and transferring property. Where there is important property to protect do not try to do this alone. Seek expert help. If you do not know who was advising the deceased, contact your own lawyer, or find a new one, to help you.

Welcome Small Gestures of Support and Comfort

Death often leaves people feeling confused. They don't know how to react, how to help, how to support those who are bereaved. They often say things like, "Call me if you need anything." But many people who are grief-stricken don't have the presence of mind to ask for help and often don't want to burden others.

People familiar with death understand that small gestures of support and comfort mean a great deal. Welcome them. If someone offers to take the dog for a walk, great. If someone offers to mow the lawn, or shop for groceries, or pick up people at the airport, welcome the help and support. If people ask what they can do, suggest a bouquet for the funeral. Also welcome friends who simply sit with you and listen to whatever you need to say.

On the other hand, some people become so helpful that you begin to feel smothered. In that case, don't hesitate to tell them gently that you and your immediate family need some time with no visitors and that they should please come back another time.

Be Prepared for Insensitivity

At death-related gatherings, most people say, "I'm so sorry," or that the person "will be missed," or that the death "is a great loss for us all." Acknowledge condolences with a simple, "Thank you," or by saying, "I know you meant a lot to each other."

But the shock of death unhinges some people to the point where they feel paralyzed and simply do nothing. They may not acknowledge the death and may skip the funeral. Later, if you confront them, they may say things like, "I didn't know her that well," or "I thought it was just for family," or "I felt I'd be in the way." Such insensitivity is rarely malicious but rather a reflection of their discomfort with mortality. Try not to feel hurt. Try to forgive them.

Meanwhile, the shock of death makes other people forget social graces. They might say things like, "She should have quit smoking," or "He owed me $5,000" or "I'm surprised so many people turned out." Again, such gaffes are rarely malicious, but even if they are, try to be gracious. If someone acts inappropriately to the point where it becomes disruptive, ask a few family members or close friends to intervene and, if necessary, escort the offender from the gathering.

Begin Certifying the Death

This is the executor's first major responsibility. From now until the estate is fully distributed and the final taxes are paid, you're the person in charge and legally responsible for everything.

Executors need copies of the death certificate—lots of them—to close out the person's life (more on this in Chapter 4). If the death occurs in a hospital, hospice, or skilled nursing facility, the staff doctor on duty can sign the death certificate. If the death occurs elsewhere, contact the person's physician and ask the doctor to come to the place of death or to meet you at the funeral home to sign the certificate. Or call the county coroner. The coroner is an employee of the county in which the person died. The coroner's office and phone are listed under county government Web sites and phone directories.

If the Person Is an Organ Donor
or Arranged for Whole-Body Donation,
Follow through with Those Arrangements

Organ donation provides major social benefits. Viable donor organs are a very scarce resource, and the need for donated organs is enormous. Only profound religious prohibition should stand in the way of donation.

If you're on the fence about organ donation, be prepared to

face substantial pressure from hospital staff and organ banks to donate as many organs as possible. Everyone who cares for the dying knows the enormity of the need and the scarcity of donor organs.

There are two ways to donate human remains—organ donation (kidneys, eyes, heart, etc.) or whole-body donation ("giving your body to science").

Donor organs can only be taken ("harvested") immediately after the donor dies. Did the person opt for organ donation? Check the driver's license. In most states, driver's licenses specify whether the license holder is an organ donor. In addition, many states include organ donation specifics in the advance medical directive/power of attorney. Check there, too.

Similarly, medical schools need a steady supply of whole bodies for gross anatomy classes to train future physicians. If the person opted for whole-body donation, you may know which medical school the person selected, or the person may have left instructions in the vicinity of the will and other death-related documents. You might also check with the Anatomy Gifts Registry at www.anatomicgift.com to see if the person registered there.

If you don't know the person's intentions regarding organ or whole-body donation, the decision rests with the family and ultimately with the executor. The various religions have different views regarding organ donation. If you'd like religious guidance, contact a member of the clergy.

If the death takes place in a hospital, hospice, or nursing home, you'll probably encounter an organ bank representative.

If the person has specified organ donation or if you decide to donate organs, there is no cost to the donor's family; all you do is sign a consent form. However, most state laws require harvesting in an operating room, so if the person dies at home or in a hospice, transportation to a hospital must be arranged.

Most organs, other than eyes, bones, and certain muscular-skeletal items, must be removed and transplanted within hours of death. As living tissue, critical organs need a flow of red blood cells and the oxygen it contains to remain viable. A heart is viable for less than six hours after removal and must be preserved in temperature-controlled liquid. A kidney can last in similar conditions for 24 to 36 hours. Most states have complex regulations governing when and where harvesting and storage of donated tissue is permitted.

If transportation of the body is necessary, it's against the law for you to do it. Most state laws restrict the transport of human remains to medical personnel and mortuaries. If the organ bank transports the body, there is usually no charge. If the mortuary transports the remains to the ER, expect to be charged around $100.

For more on organ donation, visit LifeSource at www.lifesource.org/donation or OrganDonor at www.organdonor.gov.

Ask about an Autopsy

Autopsies are examinations to determine the cause of death. These days, they are performed only if medical or law enforcement authorities suspect foul play or a public health risk or want to confirm that what appears to have been a suicide really was one. But foul play is rare, and as a result, so are autopsies. They are not required if the medical personnel present decide that the death occurred naturally.

If an autopsy is required, allow the authorities to perform it. You don't pay for the autopsy; the state does.

If an autopsy is required, the body may be embalmed. Religions that ordinarily prohibit embalming, for example, Orthodox Judaism, make an exception if police authorities suspect homicide and order an autopsy.

If a medical professional suggests that an autopsy might be necessary, that person calls the county coroner, who takes possession of the remains. Cooperate with the coroner and any other law enforcement personnel you encounter.

Autopsies typically take a day or so, but toxicology reports can take up to two weeks.

After the autopsy, the body is sewn up and "released" to the family; you must call the mortuary and have the body picked up. Remember, you are not permitted to transport the body yourself.

Murder, Accidents, and Suicide

If the person was killed by a robber, an unknown assailant, or a drunk driver, there is likely a crime involved, and therefore the police will be involved. Also, in many states, a suicide must be investigated as a potential homicide, so police are frequently involved in these cases, too. When someone dies because of a car accident or a plane crash, there may not be a criminal act but there may be a tort; in other words, someone may be liable for the death because of negligence or intentional misconduct.

If a crime occurred, you should do what the police and the district attorney recommend. They may need to take possession of the body and collect other evidence as well.

If there is any chance that the death occurred because of the negligence of a third party—such as a doctor who killed a patient in the operating room or the driver of the car that hit your mother—then you need to take steps to collect and preserve evidence.

These steps include taking photos, getting the names of all witnesses and parties to the event, and interviewing people and the police. You should also consult a lawyer. Personal injury lawyers are very adept at hiring, at their expense, investigators to collect all the evidence as quickly as possible. Most personal injury lawyers charge a contingency fee, meaning that you do not pay for the lawyer until the case settles. Lawyers typically charge between 30 percent and 40 percent of the amount you win when the case is settled.

If a serious accident occurred or you suspect someone of causing the death through negligence, you should consult with a lawyer immediately.

If the Remains Must Be Shipped Elsewhere, Arrange for Shipping

If the death occurs within driving distance of the mortuary, arrange transportation through the mortuary—and brace yourself for the cost.

If the death occurs too far away to drive, then your best option is air freight. Unfortunately, most commercial airlines take terrible advantage of the bereaved by charging a fortune to fly bodies. One leading carrier quoted a price of $700 to fly human remains from Los Angeles to New York at a time when the average price for a one-way ticket for a living person was about one third of that. Shipping a body to another country can cost thousands. In addition, most states prohibit transporting bodies by air unless they've been embalmed or cremated, which adds to the cost.

If deaths occur abroad, you must contact the U.S. Embassy or the nearest consulate to make transportation arrangements.

Arrange Care for the Person's Children, Pets, and Yard

Soon after having children, most parents arrange guardianship and designate the people who will raise them if both parents die before the kids have reached the age of eighteen. Typically, guardianship documents are included in or attached to the person's or couple's will or estate plan. But in the immediate aftermath of a death, what children need most is compassionate temporary shelter and care from someone they know, someone who is available and equipped to provide such shelter and care. Permanent arrangements can be worked out later.

The same goes for pets. Your goal is to arrange for compassionate temporary care for a few weeks. Some wills specify who gets the pets or provide funds for their care. (Some people leave fortunes for pet care.) Most states have rules and forms for making legally binding gifts or bequests to pets. For example, California allows trusts to be established for pet care.

If the person has a yard or garden, arrange for its maintenance, watering, and lawn care. A dead lawn makes the house look blighted. If a family member eventually moves in, a neglected lawn will require a great deal of work to resurrect, and if you sell the house, blighted grounds will reduce its value. Hire a gardener. Or perhaps someone in the family or a friend would be willing to care for the grounds for a few weeks.

Finally, was the person legally responsible for other people as a legal guardian or conservator? If so, you need to inform the court or other authorities and make arrangements for a successor—and also make sure those in the person's care are temporarily taken care of.

File a Change-of-Address Form with the Post Office

To keep mail from piling up, file a change-of-address form with the Post Office. Typically, mail gets forwarded to the executor, who needs it to pay the person's final bills. If the mail is being forwarded to you, inform your letter carrier that you will be receiving mail for the person who has died.

Do *not* tell the Post Office that the person has died. If you do, to have the mail forwarded you'll have to present a death certificate and other evidence that you can legally receive the person's mail. Just quietly file a change-of-address form. It's much simpler.

Obtain Two to Three Dozen Original Copies of the Death Certificate

Death certificates are legal documents that bear the county (or state) seal and contain county coroners' *original* signatures. Only county governments can issue death certificates—usually the county where the death occurred.

Obtaining death certificates is one of the most important services that mortuaries provide. Death certificates are vital, because every institution you contact will need an original signed copy to certify that the death really happened: banks, other financial institutions, credit card companies, the Post Office, the Veterans Administration, pension providers, Social Security, the realtor who sells the person's property—everyone!

Order at least twenty-four, and if the person was affluent (meaning more property and more accounts at more financial institutions), order thirty-six. You need *original signed copies of the death certificate*, that is, certificates signed by the county coroner. It's not at all unusual or impolite to ask for three dozen original copies. Coroners know how important death certifi-

cates are and understand that it's their job to sign them, no matter how many the family requests.

While you're dealing with the mortuary, the staff is happy to
obtain death certificates. You'll be charged a fee, but typically it's
the same as the fee the county charges—one of the few instances
where mortuaries don't take financial advantage of the bereaved.
But after the funeral, don't expect mortuary staff to provide
much help. If you need more certificates, you must obtain them
from the county. This is a needless, time-consuming chore. It's
much easier to obtain death certificates—*two or three dozen
original signed copies*—through the mortuary.

What if you run out? Some financial institutions accept
a copy of the original death certificate provided that you also
show them the original in person. Check with the institution.

Pay the Mortuary

Mortuaries are businesses. They are skilled at providing comfort and service, but they also expect to be paid. Many require
proof of ability to pay up front—a credit card, for example—
with full payment due by the time of the funeral.

The deceased is supposed to pay, but if the estate can't cover
the cost, and if no third party pays, then it's up to you. A simple cremation costs around $2,000. Funerals generally start at
around $5,000 and go up from there. How do you come up with
the money for the funeral? The easiest way is to use a credit card,
which defers the bills for several weeks.

In the case of an elderly deceased, if you say you won't have the funds until the estate is settled, the mortuary may defer payment if you sign a sheaf of promissory notes agreeing to pay (with interest) as soon as the estate is settled. In the case of a young person unlikely to have much of an estate, the mortuary expects payment immediately.

If the person belonged to a memorial or burial society, that group will have contracts with mortuaries to provide funerals at reasonable cost.

If the person served in the military, the Veterans Administration (VA) offers burial benefits. Contact the VA at 1-800-827-1000 or www.cem.va.gov. Some unions and some occupations (e.g., police and fire departments) also help defray funeral costs. Check with the person's union or employer.

Some people have funeral insurance. It's not common, but you should check. Of course, it may not be easy to collect the money from the insurer. You may need an attorney.

You *do not* have to pay for the mortuary or a funeral. If you choose not to pay, normally the local government pays to cremate the body. The term "pauper's grave" refers to a burial paid for by the city or county.

Burial or Cremation?

If you opt for burial, every state has human disposal laws that require interment in licensed cemeteries. Some states' laws also obligate you to bury the person's remains within a certain period of time. Tropical and subtropical locales require rapid burial because heat accelerates decomposition, posing health risks to the community. And some states have unique burial laws; for example, in parts of Louisiana, corpses must not be buried in the ground—it's too marshy, and bodies can rise to the surface. Raised crypts are required.

However, human disposal laws do not pertain to cremation remains. Cremation ashes are sterile and carry none of the disease-transmission risks of decomposing corpses.

Ashes may be dispersed anywhere, except where "refuse dumping" is prohibited, for example, in streams, lakes, parks, and so on. But when the refuse is human ashes, antidumping laws are rarely enforced, not to mention that the quantity is small and rarely noticed.

When considering where to dispose of cremation ashes, it's smart *not* to broadcast your intentions. If you mention a park or some other public place where dumping is not allowed, someone might object and alert the authorities. Keep your plans to yourself; share them only with close family and friends who are invited to the event.

For Burials, Purchase a Grave Site

There are four types of cemeteries:

1. **National cemeteries** owned by the federal government are open to military veterans and their dependents. Visit the Department of Veterans Affairs Burial and Memorial Benefits Web site at www.cem.va.gov to secure burial flags, schedule a burial, and learn more about national cemeteries in your area.
2. **Public cemeteries** are owned by cities or counties and are open to residents. Contact city or county offices.
3. **Religious cemeteries** are owned by faith groups and are open to members of the religion. Contact a clergy member or religious institution.
4. **Commercial cemeteries** are open to anyone. Look in the Yellow Pages under "Cemeteries" or search the Internet.

There are three types of cemetery real estate:

1. A **grave** is a single burial space.
2. A **plot** contains space for several graves. A family plot contains enough space for many members of a family.
3. A **crypt** or **vault** is a monument, either aboveground or underground, that contains space for many people's remains.

Prices differ widely, depending on geographic location, the location within the cemetery (hilltops cost more), and your choice of a single grave, a plot, or a crypt. Single grave sites generally start at around $1,000.

In previous generations, many middle-class and affluent families purchased family plots. Nowadays, this is less likely. But it's quite possible that the person has a grave site reserved in a family plot. Examine the person's papers or talk to older relatives who might know.

To Avoid Theft during the Funeral, Arrange for Someone to House-Sit the Person's Home

If you post a funeral notice in a newspaper, on Facebook, or anywhere else, *do not* specify the date and time. Burglars (who are sometimes unscrupulous neighbors) can read the notice, and while the family is attending the funeral, the thieves can ransack the home.

As we were writing this book, a car ran a red light and crashed into a Northern California family's van. Everyone in both vehicles was killed. The story was widely covered in the media—and thieves cleaned out the deceased family's home immediately after the accident was reported in the paper and before out-of-town family arrived at the home.

A funeral notice should simply announce that a memorial has been arranged and that anyone interested in attending should contact you. Provide a phone number and e-mail address. If you must publicly announce the funeral date and time, find someone to house-sit the person's home. That's a good idea even if you've been discreet about the date and time.

3

The Days after the Death:
Nonfinancial Issues

CHECKLIST

☐ What kind of funeral did the person want?

☐ Decide religious issues.

☐ For religious funerals, arrange the appropriate officiant.

☐ Arrange postfuneral activities.

☐ Write several obituaries.

❑ Close the person's Facebook page.

❑ Consider inviting family and close friends to take keepsakes.

❑ After the funeral, expect a wave of intense grief.

❑ If you want a memorial, organize it.

❑ Consider grief counseling.

WHAT KIND OF FUNERAL DID THE PERSON WANT?

When deaths are anticipated (e.g., people who die after a long battle with cancer), people often prearrange their funerals. Ask family and close friends if the funeral has been arranged (and paid for).

If nothing has been prearranged, but you know what the person wanted, or if you're in possession of written instructions (I want a funeral mass and cremation, I want to be buried next to my husband, etc.) you're under a moral obligation to do as the person specified. But you have no *legal* obligation to follow the person's instructions. If the person wanted a huge funeral with a jewel-encrusted casket, but you opt for a modest affair, that's between you and your conscience. If you don't know what the person wanted, you must make those decisions, probably in concert with family members and perhaps close friends.

Decide Religious Issues

Religion often becomes important around the time of a death. If the person expressed a desire for a religious funeral or if that's what you and the family want, contact the appropriate member of the clergy as quickly as possible. A clergy member can help you ensure that the funeral includes the rituals the person wanted— or that the family desires. Clergy can also recommend mortuaries sensitive to religious beliefs and faith-affiliated cemeteries.

There are two major religious considerations: the timing of the funeral and the rituals to be included. Some religions have strict rules about the timing of bidding farewell to the dead. For example, Judaism specifies burial as quickly as possible (but not on the Sabbath), though rapid interment may mean that far-flung relatives and friends can't be present. Other religions embrace their own traditions about timing. Contact the appropriate clergy member, ideally shortly before the death or immediately after.

In addition, all religions have specific funeral rituals. For instance, Catholic funerals often include a wake—a time for family and friends to gather and grieve at the home or at the mortuary with the prepared body present.

If the person left no instructions or you don't know what type of funeral the person wanted, it's often best to go with the rituals of the person's family religion, with a member of the clergy officiating. At the funeral, mourners will expect it.

For Religious Funerals,
Arrange the Appropriate Officiant

Perhaps one particular clergy member comes to mind: the minister, priest, or rabbi who attended to the person's spiritual needs for many years. In that case, the officiant does not need to be briefed about who the person was. But quite often, the person and family have no relationship with a member of the clergy, and must take potluck with an officiant whose only real qualification besides religious office is availability.

This can often feel awkward, especially if the officiant says something like, "I didn't know the person, but . . ." To make everyone as comfortable as possible, it's important to acquaint the clergy member in advance with who the person was, the unique joys and challenges the person faced in life, and anything else that's pertinent about the role the person played in the family and community.

If the person was a member of a religious institution and that institution's clergy member officiates at the funeral, there may be no charge—but a donation is typically appreciated. If the officiant is some other member of the clergy, expect to pay for the officiant's services.

Arrange Postfuneral Activities

After the funeral and burial, the person's family and friends often repair to someone's home, the church social hall, or a restaurant for refreshments and more commiseration and reminiscences. If you don't want to deal with food and transportation, delegate these tasks to other people. Most folks are only too happy to help. But if you want to make the special dish the person loved and share it with everyone, that's fine, too. As we mention in Chapter 1, take care of yourself first. If you'd rather not be sociable immediately after the funeral, feel free to withdraw; you are under no obligation to entertain. People will understand.

Write Several Obituaries

Obituaries serve three important purposes. They memorialize the person, marking the end of a life. They announce the death to a broader audience than you could ever contact on your own. And the process of writing the obituary, in summing up the person's life and contributions to the lives of others, provides some comfort and begins the healing process. In addition, many obituaries specify charities designated to receive gifts in the person's memory.

Some years ago, one of my business partners suffered a cataclysmic tragedy, the death of his four-year-old son, Brendan. The boy had a heart defect that required surgery; he died on the operating table. I immediately flew across the country to my partner's home, where, as you might imagine, everyone was devastated. Relatives and friends had been called and came laden with food. Funeral arrangements were being made. What could I contribute? I gathered the immediate family and wrote Brendan's obituary. In the context of such an enormous tragedy, it was a small gesture—but one that turned out to resonate. Months later, my partner told me how much it had meant to everyone involved.

Unless the person was notable enough to merit an obituary news article, you pay for the obituary, usually by the word. Depending on the publication, this can be very expensive. The obituary for my partner's son ran in the *New York Times* and cost $4,000. In most newspapers, cost should be a few hundred dollars. Think carefully about what you want to say and weigh your words against the cost.

Where should a newspaper obituary appear? Submit the obituary to the papers serving all the communities that were important to the deceased: where the person grew up, attended college, worked, and perhaps retired. I submitted my mother's obit to the *Santa Rosa Press-Democrat* in Northern California, because that's where she lived the last twenty-five years of her life. But I also submitted versions to the paper in Palo Alto, because that's where she lived and worked for twenty years, and to the Cornell and Wellesley alumni organizations, because she'd graduated from both.

In addition, the newsletters of clubs and religious, civic, and activity-based organizations are often happy to publish extensive obituaries for free.

The best way to craft an obituary is to begin by writing a long one, one that fully summarizes the person's life, history, interests, accomplishments, and contributions to the world. Then edit it for the publications you approach—short versions for newspapers that charge by the word, and longer versions for other publications, emphasizing the person's connections to the publication's focus. Visit http://obituaryguide.com/template. php for a free obituary template.

Close the Person's Facebook Page

This is easy to do. The account of your loved one is "memorialized," in Facebook lingo. This helps to protect their privacy. Memorializing an account sets the account privacy so that only confirmed friends can see the profile or locate it in a search. Friends and family can leave posts in remembrance. When you go to reset your loved one's Facebook page to "memorialized" status, you are asked to fill out a pretty simple form and you are advised that it is solely for the reporting of a deceased person to memorialize.

Consider Inviting Family and Close Friends to Take Keepsakes

Heirs, grandchildren, and the person's friends often hope to obtain mementos to remember the person by. In the days after the death, it's too early to distribute major items: the house, car, fine jewelry, artwork, furniture, silverware, the piano, and so on. But if people have come from far away to attend the funeral or memorial, they might want to return home with a keepsake. If that's all right with you, arrange a time for selected family and friends to visit the person's home and take mementos. Or wait and give keepsakes when the rest of the person's possessions are distributed. If you allow people to take keepsakes at the time of the funeral, remove small valuables you don't want taken (jewelry, valuable art, rare books, etc.) and supervise the process.

After the Funeral, Expect a Wave of Intense Grief

While funerals honor the person who died, they also have another important function: they distract family members from their grief. Planning the funeral, making arrangements, dealing with food and accommodations, and running people to and from transportation hubs—these chores don't erase grieving, but they temporarily push it toward the back burner. For many people, the harsh finality of the person's death doesn't begin to sink in until after the funeral, when people have returned home and you're left with a huge hole in your life. Don't be surprised if you experience a postfuneral wave of intense grief.

If you have trouble sleeping, sleeping pills may help. If you remain in deep despair months after the death, then you may have slipped into depression. Consult your physician. While grieving, exercise is often emotionally helpful, exerting a calming effect and helping with appetite and sleep.

If You Want a Memorial, Organize It

Funerals formally mark the death and the disposal of the remains through either burial or scattering the ashes (or holding on to them). Funerals may be religious or secular; they may take place at the mortuary, at a house of worship, at a cemetery chapel, or at the graveside. They tend to be brief—an hour or so—and tend to feel rushed. You have to make arrangements quickly, and if the funeral is religious, you must observe specific customs and ceremonies with which you may be unfamiliar.

Memorials are more relaxed. While rarely festive, they are usually more celebratory than funerals, acknowledging the death and mourning it but emphasizing the person's *life*. Compared with funerals, memorials tend to be more secular and less formal. You're more able to shape them to your liking or organize them as the person would have wanted. They often include photos, a slide show, and possibly a video of the person's life, with family, friends, and admirers telling stories and sharing reminiscences. You rarely hear laughter at funerals, but it's more common at memorials as people recall humorous moments in the person's life. Memorials can be scheduled far enough in advance that people coming from afar can attend. They can be small and intimate or large enough to include people from all facets of the person's life.

As you arrange the funeral or shortly afterward, discuss the possibility of a memorial with family and the person's close friends and decide if you'd like one. If so, set a date and begin organizing it. Memorials typically take place a few weeks or months after the death, after the period of immediate intense grieving, and often occur at the person's home, favorite park, or even the café or bar where the person was a regular. Think about where that person would want to be right now if he were alive. That's a great spot for the memorial.

Consider Grief Counseling

After the death of your loved one, you may have trouble coping, sleeping, and returning to your everyday life. If you start to feel "stuck" in your grief, consider professional counseling or a support group. Counseling and support groups can be especially helpful in cases of traumatic death: murder, suicide, an animal attack, being swept out to sea, and events of these kinds. To find a grief counselor, ask your physician, clergy, friends, or a social worker. If the death was a suicide, contact Survivors of Suicide at www.survivorsofsuicide.com. If the death was violent, contact Parents of Murdered Children at www.pomc.com.

4

The Days and Weeks after the Death: Financial Issues

CHECKLIST

☐ Hire an accountant.

☐ Pay funeral expenses.

☐ If the person was employed, collect final wages and other payments.

☐ If the person received Social Security checks, stop them.

☐ Collect the Social Security death benefit.

❑ Investigate Social Security survivor benefits.

❑ Notify life insurers, the military, and other institutions that pay death benefits.

❑ Investigate pension benefits.

❑ Investigate Veterans Administration and other federal government benefits.

❑ Apply for an Employer Identification Number.

❑ Notify the Internal Revenue Service that you're the executor.

❑ Cancel the person's insurance policies.

❑ Open a checking account for the estate.

❑ Find the most recent will.

❑ Find the person's assets.

❑ A quick introduction to probate.

❑ Find the person's debts.

❑ Determine the estate's value and net worth.

❑ Wrongful Death lawsuit?

❑ Contested will?

❑ Dividing the property.

❑ Understand the three types of assets.

❑ Understand the different types of ownership.

❑ Avoid probate if possible.

❑ Distribute assets exempt from probate as specified in the will.

❑ If possible, claim assets using simple probate affidavits.

❑ If regular probate is necessary, consult an attorney.

❑ Transfer title to property, vehicles, retirement plans, and securities.

In this chapter, we answer the most frequently asked—and most important—financial questions that arise when someone dies, among them:

- How do I get immediate access to some cash so I can pay the person's bills?
- Which bills must be paid? Are there any I don't need to pay?
- What is probate? How can I avoid it?
- How do I transfer title to property?

Dealing with the money is time-consuming and complicated, but it's not terribly difficult if you approach it in an organized fashion.

Hire an Accountant

We strongly urge you to hire an accountant who has experience dealing with estate finances. These matters can be complicated, and an experienced accountant can ultimately save you a lot of wasted time, undue stress, and money. You may also need a lawyer, but you definitely need an accountant. Accountants don't come cheap, but if the person owned any property, vehicles, or a business, an accountant will spare you a great deal of hassle.

Pay Funeral Expenses

Death is costly. During the days after the person dies, you'll be faced with many absolutely necessary tasks, all of which cost money. These expenses typically start at a few thousand dollars for the mortuary, the grave site, and even costs such as changing the locks on the person's home, and so on, and may run much higher. How do you pay?

In the best of all possible worlds, the person will have made funds easily accessible by opening joint bank and investment accounts with the executor as cosigner/joint tenant (which means any owner or possessor of property. A "joint tenant" or a "tenant in common" is a person who actually co-owns property with one or more other people). In that case, the executor can freely withdraw funds from the accounts.

In the next best of all possible worlds, a family member is affluent enough to advance necessary funds until the estate can provide reimbursement (and wealthy enough to eat the expenses if the estate can't). The problem is that it can take weeks or months for life insurers to cut checks, and if the estate must go through probate, it can take many months for the court to release the person's funds and property. In the meantime, the person's pet needs food, the mortgage must be paid, the mortuary insists on payment immediately, and no doubt you have other pressing expenses as well, costs that may dwarf what you have in your own checking account. So the question becomes: How can you quickly take possession of enough of the person's money to pay the death-related expenses? And if the person had no money, can you and the family come up with enough to cover expenses?

Meanwhile, the mortuary wants $8,000 *right now*. Your sister wants the orphaned dog but can't take him for a month. You can't keep the dog at your house in the interim because your son is allergic to dog hair. The kennel wants $100 a day to house the dog. And you just received a certified letter from the bank that holds the dead person's mortgage informing you that if the missed payment isn't received in a matter of days, the bank will begin foreclosure proceedings.

For fast access to the decedent's funds, look in four places: the person's checkbook, investment accounts, credit cards, and life insurance policies, and if the person was working, the employer.

Joint Bank and Credit Union Accounts

Find the person's checkbook. Look in the decedent's desk, files, or wherever the person kept important papers. Also look at the person's computer for an accounting program such as Quicken or anything that looks financial.

How many names are on the checks? In addition to the person's name, if you see any other, and that person is alive, the living person is the cosigner/joint tenant and can write checks for any amount up to the balance.

Note: If you're the cosigner, it's inadvisable to notify the bank about the death. Banks err on the side of caution, and may refuse to release funds until ordered to do so by the probate court—even if it's a joint account. If the funds are frozen, expect them to remain frozen for several months. In the meantime, you must pay the death-related expenses.

Credit Cards

Look in the person's wallet and/or desk and files. If you find a credit card, it's technically illegal to use it. Only the person to whom the card was issued is legally empowered to use it. However, if you're using it to pay the dead person's bills or death-related expenses, and you pay over the phone, you may be able to use the card up to its credit limit. You may also be able to use the card in person—unless a vendor notices that the signatures don't match. Then you probably have several weeks before you have to come up with the funds.

Other Joint Accounts

These include investment accounts with major brokerage houses. If you're a cosigner, you can withdraw funds.

If you must spend your own funds to pay death-related expenses, keep records so the estate can reimburse you.

Don't Fear Probate

The word *probate* may intimidate you. Don't let it. Probate involves nothing more than having the court supervise the executor's distribution of the estate. Probate is a valuable process. Probate laws regulate postdeath payment of bills and transfer of money and property. If you comply with the rules—typically, an attorney helps you do this—there can be no question about the estate being distributed legally and fairly. No creditors or disgruntled relatives can pop up later and sue you or hound you for money the estate supposedly owes them. The probate court determines the validity of a will and grants it approval. Once a will becomes probated, it is a legal document, and the executor and courts have the authority to uphold it.

If the Person Was Employed, Collect Final Wages and Other Payments

If you present a death certificate, most employers will cut a check fairly quickly for payment of final wages. By law, they are required to pay the person's final wages and any accrued vacation and sick time immediately. If you think the process is taking too long, consult a lawyer.

If the Person Received Social Security Checks, Stop Them

Some people believe that Social Security checks can continue to be cashed after the person dies. It's important to realize that this is not the case.

Three months after my mother's death, Social Security was still sending payments by direct deposit into her bank account.

I don't know what I was thinking, but I believed that we, her children, would continue to receive her checks as her survivors. I called Social Security and asked the payments to be transferred into my account as executor. The person at Social Security got huffy and said, "You're breaking the law. You have to return every cent you received after your mother's death. Immediately." Within forty-eight hours, I received a blunt letter from Social Security demanding all the money back—or else. It's a federal crime to defraud Social Security by failing to inform the agency of a recipient's death.

Sometimes, mortuaries contact Social Security to register the death and terminate benefits payments, but not always. The executor must contact the agency to do this. If you don't, you're liable for interest charges, penalties, and possibly even criminal prosecution. Contact Social Security at 1-800-772-1213. You must make a phone call; as of this writing, deaths cannot be reported online.

Collect the Social Security Death Benefit

When you tell Social Security that the person has died, ask about the Social Security Death Benefit. As this book goes to press, it's $255. The benefit is paid to the surviving spouse. If there is no spouse, the benefit is paid to the beneficiary whose name appears on the person's Social Security record.

Investigate Social Security Survivor Benefits

Family members may be eligible to receive monthly survivor benefits. Qualifying survivors include:

- A widow or widower, if age sixty or older (fifty if the survivor is disabled);
- The deceased's unmarried minor children;
- Some adopted minor children, stepchildren, and step-grandchildren;
- Some divorced spouses.

If the person was not receiving Social Security, survivors may still be eligible for benefits. Check with Social Security. To collect survivor benefits, you must provide Social Security with:

- A death certificate;
- The deceased's Social Security number;
- Your Social Security number;
- Your birth certificate;
- If the applicant is a spouse, the couple's marriage certificate;
- If the applicant is a divorced spouse, the divorce certificate;
- If the applicants are dependent children or stepchildren, their Social Security numbers and birth certificates;
- The name of each applicant's bank, the routing number, and the account number for direct deposit.

Notify Life Insurers, the Military, and Other Institutions That Pay Death Benefits

If the person had a life insurance policy, notify the company. Once you provide a death certificate, life insurers are supposed to send the policy payout in a timely manner, within a month or so. However, they may not do so. Insurance companies hate to part with money, so they may send you dozens of forms that must be completed perfectly before they'll pay. If you fail to cross one T, they'll refuse to pay and may even refuse to tell you what mistake you made. Keep track of your contacts with the insurer. Log phone calls and keep copies of any letters or e-mails you send. If you have not received the death benefit in a month or two, contact a lawyer. Usually, a lawyer's letter will induce them to produce the check.

If the person served in the military, inform the Veterans Administration (VA) of the death. The VA pays a death benefit of $7,000 to $10,000.

You must also notify the financial institutions that administer the person's pension, any annuities, any lawsuit settlements, and, if the person had a reverse mortgage, the bank that holds it. If the person had a relationship with a financial advisor, you should consult him or her. In the absence of that, most banks and other institutions have departments that are equipped to help you figure things out. Remember, this may be your first time, but it's not for the institution.

Some but not all annuities provide lump-sum payouts upon death. Again, the companies may delay the payout or refuse to pay. Keep a record of your calls and correspondence. If you get fed up, contact a lawyer.

If the person had a reverse mortgage, the estate may still have some equity in the property. Contact the bank that holds the mortgage.

Investigate Pension Benefits

Many pensions provide ongoing partial benefits to surviving spouses. They may also include a one-time death benefit. Examine the person's pension documents carefully. When in doubt, contact the pension program administrator.

Investigate Veterans Administration
and Other Federal Government Benefits

If the person was receiving VA benefits, the surviving spouse may be eligible to receive them. Contact the VA at 1-800-827-1000. If the person was a current or past federal government employee, survivors may be eligible for benefits. Contact the Office of Personnel Management at 1-888-767-6738 or http://www.opm.gov.

Apply for an Employer Identification Number

Between the time of the death and the final distribution of the estate, the person's assets—bank accounts and other investments—are likely to earn some income. Taxes must be paid on interest and other income, and to pay these taxes, you need an employer identification number (EIN), basically, a Social Security number for a business. To obtain an EIN, contact the Internal Revenue Service at 1-800-829-4933 or http://www.irs.gov. Or work with an estate attorney.

Notify the Internal Revenue Service
That You're the Executor

When you handle other people's money, you enter into a "fiduciary" relationship with them. A fiduciary relationship involves lots of laws focused on preventing fraud. The first is that fiduciaries must register with the government. You must file IRS form 56, "Notice Concerning Fiduciary Relationship," available at http://www.irs.gov/pub/irs-pdf/f56.pdf. To file this form, you must include the estate's EIN.

Cancel the Person's Insurance Policies

If the person had health or dental insurance, cancel those policies. As soon as the person's car is sold or bequeathed, cancel the auto insurance. As soon as the person's home or other insured assets have been distributed, cancel those policies. It's possible you may be due a refund. Ask.

Open a Checking Account for the Estate

You'll need:

- The estate's employer identification number;
- A copy of the death certificate;
- Proof that you're the executor;
- A copy of your photo identification.

Once this account is opened, use it *exclusively* to receive all of the deceased's assets, pay all bills, and distribute all assets. Settling the person's affairs is much easier when everything flows into and out of one bank account.

Records to Locate

❑ Social Security records

❑ Tax returns

❑ W-2 forms or 1099 forms (showing wages)

❑ Online investment accounts

❑ Investment records

❑ Life insurance policies and premium payment records

❑ Annuity policies

- ❏ Bank statements

- ❏ Brokerage account statements

- ❏ Business agreements: LLCs, partnerships, stock certificates

- ❏ Checkbooks

- ❏ Child support documents

- ❏ Credit card statements

- ❏ Divorce (including property settlement agreements) and prenuptial agreements

- ❏ Health insurance policies

- ❏ Immigration and citizenship documents

- ❏ Birth certificates

- ❏ Military service records

- ❏ Pension records

- ❏ Real estate deeds

- ❏ Registration papers for vehicles or boats

- ❏ Retirement account statements

- ❏ Workers' compensation or disability claims

Find the Most Recent Will

A valid will is crucial. It determines who gets what. But that's *all* it does. It does not pay the person's debts, allocate funds to pay them, or determine if probate is necessary. A will simply appoints an executor to distribute what remains of the estate after the bills are paid, and tells the executor how to distribute it. Wills may contain general bequests, for example, "Fifty percent of my assets go to my wife, Mildred," and may also contain specific bequests, for example, "Edward gets my boat."

Wills may also *exclude* people from inheritance: "To my drug-addicted daughter, Martha, I leave nothing except a two-week voucher for the Betty Ford Clinic." However, in many states, wills cannot disinherit spouses. The legal term is "spousal benefits," and in states with these benefits, no matter what the will says, the spouse is entitled to 50 percent of all net assets. Note that these laws apply *only* to spouses, not to anyone else.

Look for the will in the person's desk, files, or safe-deposit box. If you have a key, most banks allow supervised access to a safe-deposit box *solely* to inventory and photocopy the documents inside. You cannot take possession of valuable contents—jewelry, for example—until the estate is in probate, if that's necessary, or until you provide a document proving that you are the executor of the estate.

To be legally valid, wills must comply with all state law requirements, typically that they're signed, witnessed, and dated. The main exception to this rule is a "holographic" will, a document written in the person's own hand and signed. Most states deem a holographic will legally binding even if no witnesses signed it.

Look for the *most recent* will. Typically, wills state that they supersede and replace all previous wills.

If the person did not leave a will or if the will cannot be found, state probate law dictates how the property must be distributed. Ask a lawyer about the law in your state; usually the surviving spouse inherits half to all of the estate. In states where the spouse inherits less than the total amount, the children get the rest. If there is no spouse, the children inherit. If there are no children, the person's parents inherit. If the parents are deceased, the person's siblings inherit. If there are no living siblings, those who can prove that they are blood relatives inherit. And if no relatives step forward, the person's estate reverts or, in legal terms, "escheats," to the state.

If the person never married or married only once, chances are you're looking for one will or maybe one or two others that over time superseded the original. But if the person married more than once and had children with more than one spouse, then things can become complicated, and you might encounter multiple wills and perhaps several codicils—amendments that may or may not be attached to the most recent will. Save every will you find. Present them to the estate's attorney.

If the decedent had no will or if no will can be located, then the person died "intestate." Consult a lawyer.

Find the Person's Assets

Okay, you've already found some assets: the checking account, credit cards, and so on. Now it's time to find the rest of the deceased's net worth: deeds to property, motor vehicle titles, bank statements, and documentation pertaining to ownership of life insurance policies, pensions, stocks, bonds, mutual funds, annuities, and other investments. This can get complicated. Try to relax, go slowly, and take lots of deep breaths.

Finding all the assets is important for two reasons: their total value is key to the estate's net worth, which determines whether it must be probated, and if so, which type of probate. And the heirs are, no doubt, interested in the size of the pie they'll split.

Where do you find documentation of assets? Probably in the vicinity of where you found the person's checking account and credit card information, so start there. You can also:

- Go through the person's desk, files, attic, and basement;
- If the person had a safe-deposit box, find the key, and with a death certificate, you should be able at least to see what's inside it;
- Ask family members and close friends where the person kept important documents;
- Check the person's federal income tax Form 1040, which lists interest and dividends and can point you to their sources, which are assets;
- Check the person's computer;

- Check e-mail records for correspondence from financial institutions;
- Your last resort is to wait until the first quarter of the year following the death, when 1099s are mailed. Institutions that manage assets must send earnings statements for April 15 tax reporting, so watch the person's mail from January through March.

Usually, as wealth increases, so does the number of financial accounts and other assets. Chances are that you have at least some idea of the person's financial situation, from no money, to a little, to more, to lots. Your understanding of the person's situation should guide your search for assets. If you know that the person resided in a home with a paid-off mortgage and lived entirely on Social Security and a pension, you don't have to obsess about assets. But if the person was more affluent and you recall conversations about investments, then it behooves you to conduct a more extensive search.

In the best case, the person was well organized and had assembled a file called something like "My Estate Plan," including documentation of all assets: the names of all financial institutions, account numbers, deeds to all properties, and documents that identify all other assets.

Unfortunately, many people with significant assets are less than optimally organized. If the person is lucid as death approaches, you might ask about assets, what the person owes, and where to find the evidence. But few people feel they can do this. It feels awkward to say, in effect: we both know you're dying, but before you go, how about telling me where all your money is? If you can't have this conversation, that's fine, you can find the assets in other ways. But if you can, it may save you time and effort.

People with investment capital tend to invest through major brokerage or investment firms. But don't overlook other possibilities, for example, private loans and entrepreneurial investments.

If the person lent money to anyone and you can find the loan agreement, the debtor's obligation to repay the loan doesn't cease when the person dies (unless the agreement clearly states that it does). Inform all debtors of the death. Then remind them that they must continue to meet their obligations. Checks should be made payable to a new name (the executor) and sent to a new address. Another approach is to offer debtors forgiveness of some portion of the loan if they pay off the rest immediately.

A Quick Introduction to Probate

After determining the person's assets, the next logical step is to determine if the person left any debts. But before we delve into that, we must mention one of the most dreaded and misunderstood elements in dealing with death: probate. Before you can distribute the estate's net assets and before you can pay off any debts, you (perhaps with a lawyer's help) must determine if the estate needs to be probated.

Probate is the court-supervised distribution of a person's

estate. Most states have special probate courts or procedures. Under probate, the court specifies the manner in which creditors are notified and paid and the distribution of the remaining assets to the person's heirs or beneficiaries. While probate is costly and time-consuming, it has the benefit of protecting the beneficiaries since a probate proceeding precludes creditors from later challenging the distribution of assets.

There are three ways an estate can be settled: no probate, simplified probate, and full probate. We discuss the implications more fully later in this chapter, but for now, here's what you need to know:

No probate. The estate is small. Its value comes in below the amount that triggers probate in your state. Or the deceased used trusts and other vehicles to avoid probate—see pages 102 8 and Chapter 6.

Simplified probate. The estate is small enough to qualify for "short-form" probate as specified by state law.

Full probate. The estate is large enough to require a court-supervised process.

Complicating matters, certain assets and debts are exempt from probate—even if full probate is required. Most important assets held in trust are exempt from probate.

Probate is a hassle, but ultimately it's beneficial. Because it's a court supervised process, once you finish with it, no creditor can ever come after the estate (or you!) for an unpaid debt.

Find the Person's Debts

Good news, bad news. The bad news is that death does not elim-inate most debts. But the good news is that there are some you're under no legal obligation to pay (see the box below).

Most important to remember is that the government never sleeps. The executor must pay all debts owed to the IRS, state taxing agencies, Medicare, and the Social Security Administration for overpayments of Supplemental Security Income (SSI).

The executor must also continue to make payments on any mortgages or motor vehicle loans (cars, boats, etc.) until the home or vehicles have been distributed to heirs, after which the recipients assume payment.

Three Important Rules about Debts

1. During the pendency of the estate proceedings, since the property remains part of the estate, and since no one wants a default on the mortgage or loan, the estate MUST keep making the installment payments to preserve the property as an asset. However, once the property can be distributed to the heirs, the heirs take the property subject to the loan. The loan balance does not need to be paid by the estate. Loans secured by property are *not* debts of the

---

estate. Whoever inherits the home assumes the mortgage. Whoever inherits a motor vehicle assumes any loan. However, a will may specify that the estate pays the mortgage.

2. With two small exceptions, only the estate is liable for the decedent's debts. The general rule is that creditors can collect only from the estate, not from the person's survivors. If people die owing more than their net worth, the creditors eat the loss. They can't come after you. Some unpaid creditors may contact you and threaten to sue you personally. Don't be intimidated. You have no liability—unless:

    a. You're the spouse and the debts were community property. If a married couple borrows money and the husband dies, the spouse must pay the debt. But consult a lawyer. If the person incurred the debt before the marriage, it may not be community property and the spouse does not have to pay. The same rule applies to debts held by joint tenants. In most states, under most circumstances, when property is acquired under joint tenancy (but not tenancy-in-common), neither the property nor the recipient is responsible for the decedent's debts. In other words, if I die, any property jointly owned by me and others in joint tenancy goes to the other owners debt-free.

b. You took assets from the estate *and* they are assets
    that creditors may claim. Let's say Dad dies, leaving his
    house, boat, collection of antique watches, and a bank
    account containing $100,000. But he owes his busi-
    ness partner $200,000. By law, to satisfy debts, many
    states provide that creditors may not seize a person's
    primary residence or personal property, so the most
    his partner can recover is $100,000. If you give him
    Dad's cash, the debt is settled. However, if you try to
    keep the money, expect his partner to sue you.

3. Credit card companies rarely make claims—unless the
    estate is in probate. Let's say Dad died years ago and Mom
    owns a house and lives on Social Security and a small
    pension. She also has three credit cards and owes $30,000
    on them. Social Security and her pension end upon her
    death. The credit card companies are legally entitled to
    pursue the estate for unpaid balances, whether or not the
    estate goes through probate. However, in practical terms,
    credit card issuers rarely pursue claims outside of probate
    unless the person's assets—especially if they are held in
    trusts—are quite large. They don't go after small estates.

    One reason is that many states have homestead
    exemptions that protect some or all of the value of a pri-
    mary residence from creditors. In Florida, it's the entire
    value of the house, which is likely why O. J. Simpson moved

there when his murdered ex-wife's parents sued him. He bought a large home and they couldn't touch it. However, in California, only $40,000 of the value of a home is exempt. Another reason is the hassle factor. Banks would waste too many resources going after people who took Mom's old television and china set.

More good news: except for mortgage debt and motor vehicle debt, the decedent's debt liability extends only to that person's assets—the heirs do not inherit the debt. If the person's debts exceed the estate's net worth, the unpaid creditors cannot sue the executor or anyone in the family for the balance.

Look for documents pertaining to auto loans, credit cards, student loans, mortgages, lines of credit, installment sale contracts, and any other promissory notes. Debts are easier to find than assets because if the death results in a missed payment, the creditors come after the money.

Pay regularly recurring bills immediately: car payments and utility, telephone, cable, and Internet bills. As you close the person's home, cancel utilities and communications services.

If the person set up automatic payments through a bank, it may be complicated to terminate them. If you're a cosigner on the person's bank account(s), the fastest way is to close the account, and then ask creditors to send any bills to your own address. If you are not a cosigner, the bank may freeze funds until the estate has been settled by probate or until you write a letter certifying that the estate is not subject to probate.

If the bank freezes funds, as bills arrive, inform creditors that they will be paid as soon as funds are unfrozen. Delayed payments may trigger penalty charges, but in cases of estates in any form of probate, many creditors forgive them. Negotiate with the creditor or consult a lawyer.

If the estate does not need to be probated, pay all other creditors promptly. Provide a death certificate, inform creditors that you will pay on behalf of the estate, and review the terms to be sure that you and the creditor agree. If you disagree, consult a lawyer.

If the estate must be probated, inform creditors that payments may be delayed by the process. For estates in probate, don't pay credit card bills or other debts until creditors file the form necessary to become "qualified creditors." You must publish a legal notice of the probate proceedings. You must also notify creditors that they must submit proof to the court that they are in fact creditors with valid claims on the estate. A probate attorney takes care of all of this.

If there's a surviving spouse, that person *must* pay the decedent's outstanding credit card debts, because spouses are legally responsible for each other's debts. But if there is no spouse and if the estate is too small for probate, credit card companies can—but typically don't—sue the person who's inherited assets from the deceased for the amount owed, but *only* to the extent of the value of the property you received from the deceased. But if the estate is in probate, credit card companies usually attempt to collect debts, even small ones.

You may feel a moral obligation to pay, but credit card companies typically write off the debts of people who die owing less than $100,000. If you send the credit card company a death certificate and a statement that says, "She died and her estate has no money to pay her credit card debt," 99 percent of the time the credit card issuer will walk away.

Why don't credit card issuers try harder to collect? Three reasons: homestead laws, family allowance laws, and public relations.

Homestead laws. Most states have homestead laws that grant some or all of the value of the person's primary residence to the surviving spouse or children and prohibit most creditors from seizing it to repay debts. Note that the IRS and state tax agencies can take possession of a primary residence to settle tax obligations, but other creditors cannot.

Family allowance laws. These laws allow families to retain enough money from the estate to continue living. The allowance is meant to help support the surviving family during the time it takes to probate the estate. The amount is determined by state law and varies from state to state.

Public relations. Credit card companies don't want to be viewed as evil. They'd rather continue collecting 20 percent or more in revolving monthly interest on millions of living people's credit card debts than risk an outcry over throwing people out of their homes to settle dead relatives' debts. This is why, for credit card debts of less than $100,000, card issuers usually walk away. We emphasize *usually*. In some cases, they may come after you. But it's unlikely.

Determine the Estate's Value and Net Worth

First, estimate the total value of the person's assets. Next, subtract the value of all assets that are *not* counted when determining the size of the estate for probate purposes. (Probate law varies from state to state, so check online to determine candidacy.) Third, check to see if the state is a "gross" or "net" asset state. For example, in Arizona, the net value of assets is used to determine if the estate must be probated. You deduct the value of all "liens and encumbrances" to arrive at the "net" asset value. If that number is less than $50,000, simplified probate is usually permitted. Check your calculations with a lawyer.

To determine the value of the home, consult a realtor or pay for an appraisal. For art, jewelry, collectibles, and businesses, you might have to hire an appraiser. If you do, the estate pays for appraisals. To find an appraiser near you, contact the American Society of Appraisers at www.appraisers.org.

Wrongful Death Lawsuit?

If the deceased person was killed intentionally or in an accident, survivors may be able to recover money for pain and suffering and to help make up the lost income the deceased person would have provided to the family. Survivors must file what's called a "wrongful death" lawsuit. Family members may win such a lawsuit if the death was caused by, for example, a drunk driver, an incompetent doctor, someone committing a crime, or a defective product such as tainted drugs or food.

Losing a loved one under any of these circumstances is exceptionally painful, and probably the last thing family members want to think about is a lawsuit. But lawsuits must be filed within a certain period after the death, and it can be important to gather evidence right away. So if you think a lawsuit may be justified, you should talk to an experienced personal injury lawyer as soon as you feel able.

Contested Will?

Only about 1 percent of wills are contested, but when this happens, it's always ugly, because the dispute involves angry family members. And as the conflict wends its way through the legal system, it gets uglier, because the process delays distributions, which typically angers family members even more.

Wills must be contested in probate court, often at considerable expense. The burden of proof that the will is illegitimate falls on the person suing, but defending the will falls on the executor, who uses estate assets to defend the challenge. This diminishes the estate, so all the heirs suffer, often loudly. However, these days, many probate courts automatically refer contested wills to mediation, which is faster, less costly, and less rancorous than court battles.

Wills may be contested on the following five grounds.

- **Mistakes or bad luck** Suppose a person with a million-dollar estate bequeaths $400,000 to each of her two children, and $200,000 to her favorite charity. Then, the day after the person dies, the stock market crashes, and the estate is worth only $500,000. The heirs cut everything in half and send the charity $100,000. But the person told the charity to expect $200,000 and the charity sues for the full amount promised. This type of dispute is almost always mediated. (Many states have "abatement" rules that govern asset distributions that turn out to be smaller than the parties expected. Typically, the family receives what was promised, or as close to it as possible, and third parties, including charities, receive less.)

- **Who inherits?** Suppose the will of a person with a large estate says it should be "divided equally among my children." Then someone shows up at the funeral who claims to be the person's child born out of wedlock. If the claim is correct, does that child inherit? Usually, yes. This type of dispute is almost always mediated.

- **Coercion** Someone coerced the person to write the will in a way that unduly favors the one bringing pressure to bear, so the will does not reflect the true wishes of the person who wrote it.

- **Legal incompetence** People who write wills must be "of sound mind." Those suffering dementia, mental illness, or severe emotional trauma are not considered to be of sound mind. A little forgetfulness or preoccupation is not enough; the challenger must prove that the person was truly incompetent.

This is the most common reason that people contest wills. Typically, near the end of the person's life, a conniving caregiver or unscrupulous lawyer persuades the person to leave money to him or her. In such cases, the burden of proof is on the family to prove mental incompetence on the part of the person and/or wrongdoing by the caregiver or lawyer.

To avoid abuse by end-of-life caregivers and attorneys, most states have very strict laws governing gifts and bequests to them. Some states require additional witnesses or an additional attorney to approve the new will. Others shift the burden of proof to recipients, who must prove that the decedent *really meant* to give them the money.

- **Fraud or forgery** If the person's signature was forged, the will is invalid. If the person signed a document not knowing that it was a new will, that will is invalid.

States require witnesses specifically so that if anyone contests a will, the witness(es) can be questioned about coercion, competence, fraud, and forgery.

Many people threaten to contest wills, but few do. One reason is that they feel hurt or disappointed that the will did not treat them or their children as generously as they expected. But hurt and disappointment are not legal grounds to contest wills. Executors should try to mollify complainers, perhaps with the help of a family meeting or professional counseling.

The other reason that wills are rarely contested is that it's very difficult for a challenger to prevail in court. If anyone threatens to contest and the family cannot resolve things on their own, consult a lawyer.

Dividing the Property

We devote the rest of this chapter to dividing the property and transferring ownership. No matter how this happens—without probate, with simplified probate, or with full probate—the process is pretty much the same. The only real difference is that with either type of probate, the division is court approved.

Understand the
Three Types of Assets

Most estates have three classes of assets: major items, household goods, and items of sentimental value.

Major items include homes and other real estate, cash, stocks, and bonds. "Real property" means real estate: houses, farms, cabins, undeveloped land, even vacation time-shares.

Personal property is everything else, including household goods, which include cars, furnishings, clothing, dishes, electronics, bikes, books, jewelry, musical instruments, art, and antiques.

Sentimental items may have substantial monetary value (your great-grandmother's silver service) or little value (the tennis trophy the person won fifty years ago).

All three types of property must be divided among heirs and beneficiaries or given away or sold, but doing this poses challenges.

Most household items, for example dishes, clothing, and furniture, can be transferred simply by taking possession of them. The old adage that "possession is nine-tenths of the law" holds true here as the *person in possession of property has a stronger claim than someone who merely says it belongs to them. But know that ownership can ultimately be challenged in court.* Most of the time, though, all of the person's household items can simply be given to the heirs. While technically part of the probate estate, few care about it. Unless someone contests ownership—two of you want Mom's pearl necklace—possession is sufficient.

However, if the estate includes a painting by Paul Cézanne or a Stradivarius violin, these "household items" will likely be regarded by the court (or creditors) as assets worthy of being considered part of the estate. Items of this nature may need to be sold and the cash generated used to pay creditors or divided among the heirs or beneficiaries. Note that the law makes a distinction between the words "heirs" and "beneficiaries." An "heir" is a person who inherits from the deceased by law with or without a will. For example, the spouse typically inherits all or a portion of the estate irrespective of whether the deceased had a will. A "beneficiary," on the other hand, is a person designated by will to inherit.

But possession can also open a can of worms. True story: Mom dies and leaves everything to her two children, one of whom is a methamphetamine addict. The addict cleans out the house and sells everything for money to buy drugs. The sister calls the police, crying "Theft!" The police say, "No, it's not theft, your mother left her estate to both of you, and your brother took what he thinks is his fair share." The sister calls a lawyer, crying, "Help!" The lawyer tells her, "I'm sorry your brother did this, but everything he seized and sold is gone. You won't get it back. Here's what you do: assign a value to everything he took and deduct it from his share of the remainder of the estate."

However, things may become complicated when legal possession depends on a document, for example, the pink slip for a car. Motor vehicles, real estate, and bank and brokerage accounts fall into this category of property. Whenever title is determined by a piece of paper, you have to deal with the government—the department of motor vehicles for cars, the county for real estate deeds—or banks or brokerage firms.

Note: The person's debts must be paid first, before the assets are distributed to heirs and beneficiaries. They get what remains after the person's debts are paid.

Major Items

The standard approach with homes, investment property, stocks, bonds, and other substantial assets is to have them appraised and then sold, with the proceeds divided among the heirs. The executor arranges for appraisals, and the estate pays for them. In most cases, the probate court appoints a third-party "referee" to determine value and settle any disputes about the assets' values.

Sometimes, one heir wants to move into the person's home,

another wants the vacation cabin, and one of the grandchildren could really use the car. The cleanest way to handle this is for the heirs to declare if they want any of the major items. Assuming no contention over hoped-for ownership, the assets get appraised or the heirs come to agreement on their monetary value, and then those amounts are charged against the total those heirs inherit.

But many families do things differently. With my mother's estate, my siblings and I identified twelve major items. We uncorked a bottle of wine and discussed who wanted what and what felt fair. One sister took Mom's silver service. Another took the china. My third sister wanted a valuable painting. And I wanted the piano. In the final division, some of us walked away with items that were more valuable than what the others received, but no one wanted them sold, everyone wanted them to stay in the family, and everyone was happy with the division.

What if someone wants the home but can't afford to buy it from the estate? Typically, the heirs decide on fair rent (check Craigslist and local realtors), and the person who moves in pays it (or pays the mortgage, taxes, and insurance), perhaps with a time limit on the rental, after which the other heirs can insist on a sale.

If the person who moved in assumes the mortgage or refinances the mortgage, he or she can transfer the property to his or her name from the estate, and the home then becomes that person's property. If the person who moved in can't afford to buy, then either the rental arrangement continues, or the home is sold, with the proceeds distributed to all the heirs.

However, *before* the title is transferred, check your state's laws regarding title transfers and property taxes. In most states, title transfers through inheritance do not trigger reappraisals for property tax purposes. But if a sale to an heir triggers reappraisal and the property has appreciated significantly, the person who acquires it gets hit with a huge tax bill. Rather than "sell" the property to one heir, the executor should transfer the title, then make arrangements for the others to be paid in cash the value of their portion of the property transferred.

Note: If a home is rented, the estate continues to own it and is responsible for maintaining it: paying the mortgage, taxes, and insurance, repairing anything that breaks, and doing normal maintenance. These responsibilities fall to the heirs, who may eventually weary of them and want to force a sale. Of course, this can cause conflict. We can't tell you how to resolve such conflicts, just that selling the big items is the cleanest way to dispose of them and that continuing to hold (and share) any major assets can cause problems.

Who Gets to Live in Mom's House? Who Has to Pay the Mortgage and Property Taxes?

In most families, the family home is the primary financial asset. When Dad dies, Mom inherits his half—she owns it. When Mom dies, her will bequeaths the home "in equal parts to her three children, Tom, Dee, and Mary, and their issue." Tom has a wife and two kids. Dee divorced and died several years earlier, leaving three children. Mary is single and has no children. So here's how the inheritance looks:

- Tom gets one third

- Mary gets one third

- Dee is deceased, so her three children split her third, getting one ninth each

Every owner—from Tom, who owns one third, to Dee's kids, who each own one ninth—has the legal right to live in Mom's house. In other words, all five heirs could move into the home—and none of them has the legal right to kick any of the others out.

Meanwhile, by law, *every* owner—all five of them—is legally responsible to pay every dollar of the mortgage, taxes, and upkeep. In other words, the law treats *every* owner as the *sole* owner.

So the five owners must agree on what to do with the house. They can sell it and distribute the proceeds in one-third, one-third, and three one-ninth shares. Or one person can buy all or part of the house, move in, and assume all or part of the expenses. Or the family can give the house to one person, or rent it to a family member or outsider, or make some other arrangement. If the family cannot agree on disposal of the home, every owner has the right to sue for sale of the property, with the proceeds distributed according to Mom's will. These issues are typically resolved during probate, and most states give executors broad leeway to decide how to treat all heirs fairly.

Personal Property

If someone wants the furniture, the china, Mom's sewing machine, or Dad's workbench and tools, you might follow the same procedure—assign values and charge them against that person's share of the estate. But how much are twenty-year-old pots and pans really worth? For household goods, most families divide things up idiosyncratically in ways that feel fair to those involved.

My family has an odd but beloved tradition of playing poker for them. We deal the cards, and the winner of each hand selects something. Then, in age order, the rest of us each make a selection. After everyone has selected, we play another hand.

Sentimental Items

After the funeral, you may have invited family members to take little keepsakes from the person's home. If you have not already done this, go ahead and do it any time after the funeral or memorial service. Once the major items and household furnishings have been assigned to various heirs or beneficiaries, then the heirs are free to distribute everything else as they wish, with the executor charged with mediating any disputes. You might invite everyone to attend a walk-through together and make their selections. Or you might select keepsakes and distribute them yourself.

Quite often, items of little monetary value can have tremendous sentimental value—and can cause great contention among heirs. For much of her life, my mother wore a beautiful gold locket containing small photos of her four children. All three of my sisters wanted it. Ultimately, we agreed that Tory had taken the fewest other assets, and we gave it to her.

We can't tell you how to divide items of sentimental value. Families have to do this for themselves. All we can suggest is that survivors behave kindly toward one another. No "thing" embodies the person who died. Your memories are your memories, whether or not you serve the Thanksgiving turkey on your mother's Wedgwood platter. Try to focus on your memories, not on things.

Understand the Different Types of Ownership

Major assets can be owned in several ways. For settling estates, the most important are individual property, community property, joint tenant with right of survivorship, tenancy-in-common, and trusts.

Individual Property

One person owns it. This is how people typically own most of their personal property.

Community Property

About half the states recognize community property, which means that property is legally owned by the two spouses communally. Deeds and titles may specify community property, but what's more important is when and how the property was acquired. In community property states, the general rule is that *all* properties (in fact, all assets) acquired during the marriage are community property. Each spouse legally owns half of the property—whether the title says that or not.

Spouses may leave their half to anyone they specify, but typically, when one spouse dies, the will leaves all community property to the surviving spouse. When a spouse inherits the other half of the community property, filing a death certificate is typically all that is required, especially if the deed already says "John and Mary Smith, as husband and wife."

Property received by a spouse by gift or inheritance during the marriage is *not* community property. Suppose a mother dies and leaves her married daughter a home. The house is not community property; it belongs to the daughter. If she wants to "donate" it to the community, she must take legal action to do so. If you find yourself in a situation like this, it's best to consult an attorney.

Joint Tenancy with Right of Survivorship

A joint tenancy is similar to community property, except that the owners are not spouses. The two people own the property together, and when one of them dies, the other person automatically inherits the dead person's share and becomes the individual owner of the entire property. Title normally reads "John Smith and Mary Jones, as joint tenants with right of survivorship" or simply "joint tenants." In this case, it is very easy to transfer title. Most states require only filing a death certificate. Some states require a notarized form and the death certificate. And because joint tenants automatically inherit, there's no probate.

Tenancy-in-Common

If property is owned by more than one person but not as community property or joint tenancy, chances are it's owned as a tenancy-in-common. Real estate partnerships are often tenancies-in-common. The deed contains the names of all the co-owners "as tenants in common." When a co-owner dies, that person's share of the property passes not to the other co-owners but rather to the decedent's heirs, as specified in the person's will. As a result, only that person's heirs may change the title. This happens during probate or by the heirs filing a death certificate and proof that they are the heirs.

Trusts

One very popular method of owning property is by placing it in trust. We discuss this in detail in Chapter 6. When property is owned by a trust, the trustee has the sole authority over the property and can sell or mortgage it.

The great benefit of a trust is that property held in trust is not subject to probate. The property passes directly to the designated beneficiaries identified in the trust.

Avoid Probate If Possible

How are the goals of paying all debts and distributing the remaining assets accomplished? The answer: probate. Probate involves court-supervised settlement of debts and distribution of residual assets. It's a public, transparent process designed to be fair to all.

So why does everyone want to avoid probate? Because it requires a lawyer, it's expensive, and it takes time, delaying distribution of the net worth, usually for four to six months but up to eighteen months—that's right, probate may last a year and a half. Ideally, you want to be legally free to distribute the estate's assets immediately without probate. In most cases, this is possible.

Probate does *not* change outcomes. While it's important to make the appropriate decision about probate, it does not affect who gets what, just the manner in which the distribution takes place—with or without court supervision. The process of distribution is the same.

How do you know if you can avoid probate? It depends on where you live and on the size of the estate. Laws in every state specify estate values that trigger probate proceedings. For example, in California, there is no probate for estates with assets of up to $100,000 in personal property and $20,000 in real estate, for a total of $120,000.

To find the trigger figures for your state, there are a number of excellent online resources. The Web sites covering all fifty states include:

Findlaw Estate Planning, at estate.findlaw.com

Estate Settlement.com, at www.estatesettlement.com

Estate Finance, at www.estatefinance.com

The Executor's Guide: Settling a Loved One's Estate or Trust, by Mary Randolph (Berkeley, CA: Nolo Press, 2010), also has terrific information, but since laws are subject to change, you should be sure to check for the latest trigger figures online.

Estates valued at less than your state's probate minimum automatically avoid probate, and the executor can distribute the assets without court supervision or approval. This is often called the "affidavit" process.

Note: When determining the value of an estate to see if probate is required, many valuable assets can be excluded:

- Wages owed to the decedent
- The person's primary residence, if it goes to the surviving spouse

- Community property, if it goes to the surviving spouse
- Property owned in joint tenancy
- Assets owned by trusts (living trusts, spousal trusts, and A/B trusts, which are trusts created by married couples in order to minimize estate taxes. To establish an A/B trust, each spouse places assets in the trust and names as the final beneficiary a person other than his or her spouse. The trust splits into two upon the first spouse's death, into trust A, the survivor's trust, and trust B, the decedent's trust.)
- Pensions and individual retirement accounts (IRAs) with specific designation of beneficiaries
- Motor vehicles
- Property located outside the state where the person lived (However, the state where the property is located may require probate.)

Once you exclude the assets listed above from the estate, for about 90 percent of Americans, the remaining net worth qualifies for no-probate distribution or simplified probate.

But remember, while avoiding probate saves time and money—no legal fees—the executor must still pay the person's debts and distribute what's left in accordance with the will. When someone dies leaving debts and assets, the law holds that before beneficiaries can "grab" the assets, all bills must be paid. This actually works to the advantage of the beneficiaries. If debts are paid before the distribution of assets, the estate's creditors can't hound the beneficiaries for money.

If the estate must pass through probate, we urge you to engage an attorney.

The 99 Percent

What about the other 99 percent—people who die without a house and without lots of money?

The vast majority of Americans die the way they were born; with virtually nothing. If a person did not have a house and had just small amounts of cash in a checking account or savings account, you don't need to do much of anything. Don't worry about a will or probate. Don't worry about paying the debts. If a person rented the home, take everything, divide the property among those who care, leave it clean, and go.

The small amounts of personal property and cash are not worth the time of creditors to pursue. You are *not* liable for the person's debts. If you want, send a notice and/or death certificate to the credit card companies and the landlord, and just walk away. Do not let them intimidate you. Ignore them!

Distribute Assets Exempt from Probate
as Specified in the Will

Even if an estate is large enough to require probate, many of its assets can be distributed *without* probate. These include:

- Personal property of little to no monetary value, such as dishes, televisions, and so on (note, this does not include items of significant use)
- Joint accounts (checking, savings, investment)
- The person's final salary or wages
- Life insurance proceeds, if there is a named beneficiary or beneficiaries
- Individual retirement accounts—IRAs, 401(k)s, and similar accounts if there is a named beneficiary or beneficiaries
- Pension plan distributions
- Employee death benefits—check with the employer if there are any
- Property held by living trusts
- Property registered as a "homestead"
- Community property
- Property held in joint tenancy
- U.S. savings bonds
- Any property registered as transfer-on-death (TOD) or paid-on-death (POD)
- Any assets held by trusts, typically a living trust, also known as a "spousal" or "A/B" trust

As mentioned above, any assets held in a trust are exempt from probate. Trusts are a key estate-planning tool. You don't have to be rich to benefit from trusts. You and your spouse can place your home and your investments in a trust, and once you do, they never have to go through probate. The heirs can take possession immediately. Everyone with assets should set up a trust. See Chapter 6.

If the estate is large enough to trigger probate, then you enter court proceedings. There are two types of probate: simple ("summary") probate, also known as the "affidavit procedure," and regular probate. With simple, summary, or affidavit probate, you or your lawyer complete the appropriate transfer forms (the affidavits), and you can usually gain access to the person's estate within a couple months. If you need an attorney, the fee should be modest. Consult a lawyer for the triggering amount in your state. If the estate requires regular probate, you must hire a lawyer who appears before a probate judge. The lawyer names an executor and explains how the heirs propose to distribute the estate.

When Can Aunt Susie Inherit Mom's Silver?

Silver service, televisions, furniture, workshop contents, boats, jewelry, art (even Picassos) are all considered personal property. Even though some pieces may be very valuable (think *Antiques Roadshow*), and although the law says they are part of the estate for repayment of debts, most people distribute them quickly right after the death, even if the rest of the estate is in probate.

High-value items of personal property are considered part of the estate and may be subject to probate. However, practically speaking, creditors do not look to personal property, unless they are Picassos, for repayment of the person's debts.

If Possible, Claim Assets
Using Simple Probate Affidavits

Twenty-eight states and the District of Columbia allow estate claims using affidavits: Alaska, Arizona, California, Colorado, Delaware, District of Columbia, Hawaii, Idaho, Illinois, Indiana, Iowa, Kansas, Louisiana, Maine, Michigan, Minnesota, Montana, Nebraska, New Mexico, North Carolina, North Dakota, South Carolina, South Dakota, Texas, Utah, Virginia, Washington, Wisconsin, and Wyoming.

There's a legally stipulated waiting period, usually a month, but in most states anyone can use this procedure, though in some it's open only to close relatives. To find the procedures in your state, check *The Executor's Guide*, search the Internet for "probate affidavit procedure in [your state]," or consult an attorney.

The affidavit procedure is quite easy: beneficiaries prepare simple statements that list what they are claiming, then they sign their statements in front of a notary public and present them to the person or institution that holds the asset.

Affidavits can usually be used to claim bank accounts, stocks, and motor vehicles—typically anything but real estate. Some states allow affidavit claims for real estate as well.

Some states provide fill-in-the-blanks affidavit forms. In some states, banks, other financial institutions, and departments of motor vehicles deal with inheritance affidavits so frequently that they provide forms. If no preprinted forms are available, check your state statutes and include the required information, the assets claimed (including account numbers), and a statement that:

1. The value of the claim does not exceed the state's simple-probate dollar maximum
2. The waiting period is over
3. No probate court proceedings have commenced
4. The person signing the affidavit is entitled to the property

When presenting affidavits to banks and any other institutions that hold the person's property, you'll also need:

1. A death certificate
2. Proof that the person owned the property, for example, bank statements or stock certificates
3. Perhaps a copy of the will

You may also have to send copies of affidavits to the state taxing agency in case any taxes are due.

In most states, employees of banks, brokerages, and other institutions that receive affidavits are familiar with the procedure and raise no objections to turning over the person's property. But to avoid being turned down, print out a copy of your state's statutes and bring it with you. If you're still turned down, consult a lawyer.

If Regular Probate Is Necessary, Consult an Attorney

Once the probate court certifies the executor, that person gains access to all of the estate's assets and is free to distribute them in accordance with the court-approved plan. However, many states now offer a streamlined probate process that resembles simple probate. Consult a lawyer about the laws in your state.

Note: During probate proceedings, you must continue to pay all regular bills as they come due: the mortgage, car payments, utilities, and so on. Other creditors—credit card companies and other debts—should not be paid until probate commences and you've been appointed trustee.

Transfer Title to Property, Vehicles, Retirement Plans, and Securities

The ownership of real estate, also known as real property, is determined by a document called a "deed" or "title." Deeds are filed ("recorded") with the county where the property is located. The only way to change ownership is by recording a title transfer, which changes the deed to reflect the property's new ownership.

Property can be owned in many different ways, among them: individually, joint tenants (spouses or other partners), community property (spouses), and tenants-in-common. Depending on the type of ownership, laws vary regarding transfers. Laws also vary from state to state. When in doubt, consult a lawyer.

Before property can be transferred, you need to know who owns it, that is, whose name is on the deed/title. To find out, you need the deed. Look for it among the person's financial papers or in the safe-deposit box. If you can't find the deed but a document turns up with the name of the title company or the bank that holds any mortgage, contact those institutions; they may have a copy. Or visit the county offices and request a copy of the deed. Or order a preliminary title report from a title company.

Transferring Title of Jointly Held Property

Property held in joint tenancy or as community property with right of survivorship automatically passes to the surviving owner. There is no need for probate. However, the title must be "cleared," that is, the deceased owner's name must be removed from the deed and tax records.

Rules governing title clearance vary from state to state. Consult an attorney in the state where the property is located. However, to clear a title, most states require the following documents:

- A certified copy of the death certificate
- A notarized statement in which the surviving owner declares: "I am the surviving owner of this jointly held property and now it belongs entirely to me"
- A legal description of the property (from the deed)

These documents must be filed with the land records office of the county where the property is located (the county recorder or registrar of deeds). For more on transferring property, consult the *Executor's Guide* (see page 103). When in doubt, consult an attorney.

What If the Title Wasn't Cleared after a Previous Death?

Say your parents owned their home jointly. Your father died. Years later your mom dies—and you realize that the title was not cleared after your father's death. You must do that now. If you still have a death certificate for your dad, the process is the same; it doesn't matter how long ago he died. If you no longer have any copies of the death certificate for him, consult a lawyer.

Transferring Title to Vehicles

If the vehicle was owned in joint tenancy or as community property with right of survivorship, it passes to the surviving owner without probate. But you still have to transfer the title.

Rules vary from state to state, but most require:

- A copy of the death certificate
- The title to the vehicle
- The vehicle's registration

Visit the department of motor vehicles, fill out a few forms, and pay a small transfer fee. A new title will be sent to you.

Claiming Funds in Retirement Plans

Retirement plans—401(k)s, IRAs, and similar investments—generally cannot be owned by living trusts. When people sign up for retirement plans, they almost always name a beneficiary. That person can claim the money without probate. Contact the plan administrator or the brokerage firm that hosts the plan. Present a death certificate and identification, and you can collect the funds. However, if the person did not name a beneficiary, or if the beneficiary is deceased, the money becomes part of the estate, and the executor must claim it for distribution to the estate's heirs. Contact the financial services company holding the 401(k) assets or an attorney.

Funds distributed from 401(k)s, IRAs, and other retirement plans are taxable. Be prepared to pay federal and state income taxes on distributions.

Funds held in IRAs—but *not* 401(k)s—may be rolled over into a spouse's IRA without paying taxes. Other heirs, for example, children, may roll IRA funds into "inherited IRAs." There are strict, complicated rules governing inherited IRAs—talk to an accountant or tax attorney—but if it's a large IRA, this may be a good idea.

Transferring Securities: Stocks, Corporate and Municipal Bonds, and Brokerage Accounts

There are two ways to own stocks and bonds. Most investors buy shares in mutual funds that invest in a large array of them. But some hold individual stocks and/or bonds. Mutual funds are popular because they spread risk and allow easier trading and redemption.

No matter how the person owned the securities—as mutual fund shares or individual stock and bond certificates—if the assets are held by a living trust, they are owned not by the person but by the trust. When the person dies, the trust's trustee controls them and can distribute them as part of the estate.

Brokerage firms deal with the deaths of account holders routinely. Call or e-mail the firm; it's usually fairly easy to connect with a person who can walk you through the transfer process. It typically requires a letter of instruction from the trustee telling the brokerage to release the funds or transfer them to other accounts. Letters of instruction must be "signature guaranteed," which is similar to notarized signatures except that you don't go to a notary public; instead you visit your bank, and an official there witnesses your signature and guarantees it using a stamp similar to a notary's.

If the person died in possession of jointly held stock certificates, they must be reissued in the surviving owner's name. Do this by contacting the transfer agent of the corporation that issued the stock. If the stock is publicly traded, the transfer agent is specified on the stock (or corporate bond) certificate. If the stock is not publicly traded, contact the company.

You'll have to send the transfer agent the following documents:

- A letter of instruction specifying what you'd like to do
- The original stock and/or bond certificate(s)
- A certified copy of the death certificate
- A stock "power" signed by the surviving co-owner. The "power" document authorizes transfer of the shares. It may be printed on the back of the shares, but if not, stock and bond power forms are available from banks or brokers or their Web sites. Power forms include your name, address, Social Security number, the type of stock (common or preferred), the name of the company, and the stock number (printed on the certificate). A signature guarantee is required
- A signed, notarized affidavit of residence that specifies the executor's address and where the deceased owner resided. This must be notarized

Most corporate and municipal bonds are handled the same way. Some people own "bearer" bonds of U.S. Savings Bonds. These bonds are not registered. The person in possession of them is deemed the owner. All you do is present the bond, and the issuer is required to pay the "bearer."

Who Pays for Shipping?

Let's say Mom dies in Iowa, but the son who wants the grand piano lives in California and has no intention of renting a truck and driving 2,000 miles to pick up the piano. Big items can be very expensive to ship. Typically, recipients want the estate to pay for shipping, and some wills make provision for this. If not, it's up to the executor. The estate is free to pay if the executor approves it. But once assets are assigned to new owners, legally they are no longer part of the estate. They belong to the recipient, and that person is responsible for them.

The exception is pets. If the dog must be shipped across the country, the estate pays, because by taking the pet (and the associated costs of taking care of it), the new owner is doing the estate a favor.

5

The Year after the Death

<table>
<tr><td>

CHECKLIST

❏ Take your executor's fee.

❏ Prepare to pay any taxes owed.

❏ Trusts and taxation.

❏ When are taxes due?

❏ Where does the tax money come from?

❏ Surviving spouses: special rules.

❏ It's best to work with a tax expert.

❏ If you want a grave marker, purchase and place it.

❏ Officially terminate your role as executor.

</td></tr>
</table>

Take Your Executor's Fee

By now you've realized that it's not easy being an executor. There are dozens of tasks to accomplish, and they take considerable time and effort. They may also land you in hot water with some relatives. Meanwhile, states have a compelling interest in the orderly distribution of deceased individuals' estates. So most states have laws granting executors a fee for services rendered.

Most states calculate the fee as a fixed percentage of the estate's value. Some states specify a sliding scale based on the value of the estate—a smaller percentage for large estates. In my case, my mother's estate was worth about $1 million, and California specifies an executor's fee of 2 percent, so I was awarded $20,000.

Some executors say, "Oh, I don't need the money. Let's just divide up everything equally." You're free to do this if you wish, but if you consult an estate lawyer, don't be surprised if the attorney insists that you take the fee. Why? Because it suggests that the executor took that responsibility seriously and followed the law. Of course, executors who take the fee can then share it with other heirs or do anything they wish with it. After my mother's estate was distributed, I gave my fee to charity.

Executors must declare the fee they receive as income and pay income taxes on it.

Prepare to Pay Any Taxes Owed

Tax issues are very complicated. Nearly everyone and every entity may be liable for some form of tax. Let's look at each individually.

Does the deceased owe taxes? If the deceased had income prior to death, but during the year of his or her death, then the deceased may owe income tax. If Social Security provided all of the person's income, chances are no taxes are due. But if the person received Social Security and in addition had other income—income from working, a pension, or investments—a tax obligation is likely. Even if the person owes no taxes, a refund is still possible, but it can be obtained only if you file a return.

Taxes are due on April 15 of the year after the person's death. Use the standard IRS Form 1040, but write "Deceased" and the date of death across the top of all tax forms. File using the person's Social Security number, not the estate's Employer Identification Number. If you're a surviving spouse, after your signature, write "filing as surviving spouse" and leave the other signature line blank. If you sign as the executor, write John Smith, "executor of the estate of Jane Smith." When in doubt, check with the IRS or an accountant or tax preparer.

Do the heirs or beneficiaries owe taxes? In general the answer to this question is "no." This is good news for all of us baby-boomers! In general, all of the assets that beneficiaries receive—including cash—are tax-free. You have no obligation to disclose amounts or property inherited on your tax return.

The major exceptions to this rule are distributions of IRAs, retirement accounts, and other assets categorized as "income in respect of a decedent," or "IRDs").

If you receive money from an IRA or other retirement accounts, then much of that money is treated as ordinary income. This is because the deceased person deferred taxes when he or she was alive and the IRS, therefore, expects the beneficiaries to pay the deferred income taxes on the money held in the IRA or other retirement accounts. The distribution will be reported to the IRS, so you must declare it on your tax return.

While the federal government does not tax money and other property received from an inheritance, some states do. You should check with the state in which you, as the heir, live to determine if they are due.

Does the estate owe taxes? Although the heirs don't pay taxes, except in the case of money distributed from an IRA, the estate may have to pay both federal and state estate taxes and, separately, may have to file income tax if the estate made money between the person's death and the settlement of the estate. Death taxes, or estate taxes, are taxes due to the federal and state authorities on the basis of the value of the estate at time of death. As most readers know, estate taxes are very controversial. Many people have argued that accreted wealth should not be taxed. Under President George W. Bush, the estate tax was reduced and the threshold amount or value of an estate before an estate is subject to tax was greatly increased. As a result of the changes made under President Bush, in 2010, there was no estate tax.

In 2012, the estate tax is 35 percent of the value of all assets in an estate in excess of $5.12 million. As of the writing of this book, in 2013, unless Congress changes the law, the estate tax will revert to the 2001 tax rate. That means that the value of all assets in an estate in excess of only $675,000 will be taxable at 55 percent. Also, under the "marital exemption," married couples may inherit an unlimited amount tax-free. This benefit is not currently available to married gay couples because of the Defense of Marriage Act, passed by the United States Congress at the urging of conservative Republicans in 1996, which denies the "marital exemption" to gay couples even if they are legally married in their state.

Many states also impose estate, or "death" taxes with varying exempt amounts.

For questions about estate taxes, consult a tax attorney or accountant.

Even if no estate tax is due, if the estate generates income after the death, the estate must still file state and federal tax returns. If the estate stays in existence for more than a few months and the assets in the estate earn money, then the estate most likely will need to get a tax ID number and file income tax returns at both the state and federal level. Remember, you may need to file a return even if no taxes are done.

Trusts and Taxation

We have mentioned that trusts are a great way to avoid probate. They can also be a great way to avoid estate taxes.

Most married couples write living trusts that include an A/B structure, also called a bypass trust. Here is how it works. Mary and John are a married couple. For estate and tax planning purposes they put their property in trust. When Mary dies, the trust and her will instruct John, as trustee, to split Mary's assets between the trust for John, the "A" trust, and the trust for Mary and John's children, the "B" trust. The B trust receives property whose value is less than or equal to the federal estate tax exemption (in 2012 it was $5.12 million). In other words, the money is given to the B trust tax-free. Mary's remaining assets are given to the A trust. The property transferred into the A trust is also transferred tax free under the "marital exemption," which allows a spouse to inherit all property in an estate without estate tax.

During John's lifetime, he has access to the income from the B trust and, in fact, can also spend the principal of the trust for his "health, education, support, or maintenance." In other words, even though the assets in the trust were given to their children, John has access during his lifetime.

But here is the good part. When John dies, all of the assets in the B trust are given to the children tax-free. Since they were never "owned" by John they are not part of his estate. The only estate tax due when John dies is on the assets of the A trust.

If John and Mary had not created the trusts, all of the property that Mary and John had would be subject to tax upon John's death.

Yet another benefit of the A/B structure is that the heirs, once they receive the property, also receive a step-up in basis for tax purposes. In general, under the tax law, when you sell property, you are only liable to pay taxes on the "profit" or "income" you derive. Your "cost," or basis, in the property is not taxable. For example, if you bought property for $100,000 and then sold it for $125,000, your gain is $25,000 because your "basis" was $100,000.

When Mary dies, the property transferred into the B trust is revalued at fair market value at the time of her death, meaning that when the heirs ultimately sell the property, their basis in the property is the fair market value at the time of her death rather than the price John and Mary paid for the property many years before.

When Are Taxes Due?

The dates for which taxes are due are as follows:

- Federal income tax for the final year of the person's life—due by April 15 of the year following the death
- State income tax (in most states) for the person's final year—due by April 15 of the year following the death
- Federal income tax for the estate (income on money the estate earned after the person died if the income is $600 or more)—due by April 15 of the year following the death
- State income tax for the estate—due by April 15 of the year following the death
- Federal income tax for any trusts (income on money the trust earned after the death)—due by April 15 of the year following the death

- State income tax for any trusts—due date depends on the state
- State inheritance tax (in some states)—due date depends on the state
- Federal estate tax (only the wealthiest 1 percent of Americans owe this tax)—due nine months after the death
- State estate tax—due nine months after the death

Where Does the Tax Money Come From?

From the person's estate. Surviving spouses remain responsible for the dead person's taxes, just as they were responsible for their spouse's taxes while the person was alive. But no other survivor is responsible for any decedent's taxes.

Surviving Spouses: Special Rules

A surviving spouse may file a joint return for the year of the deceased spouse's death, even though the decedent did not live the whole year. However, if the surviving spouse remarries in the same tax year, the return for the dead person must be filed as "married filing separately."

A surviving spouse with a dependent child may qualify for an income tax break for two tax years after the death. For qualifications, consult a tax advisor.

It's Best to Work with a Tax Expert

Even if you have an accountant prepare the tax returns, the executor (or the trustee of a trust) is legally responsible for making sure the taxes are actually paid properly. If you don't pay by the various due dates, you're liable for interest and penalties, and possibly even criminal prosecution.

Most executors delegate tax-preparation chores to tax professionals. Did the decedent have a tax accountant? If so, it's a good idea to consult that person. Ask relatives or the decedent's friends if they know who prepared the person's taxes. Look through the person's desk, files, or personal phone numbers. Or find the person's most recent tax returns. Accountants and other tax professionals must sign all the forms they prepare.

But if you choose, you're free to prepare the person's final tax return and the estate's return yourself. You can obtain all federal tax forms from the Internal Revenue Service at www .irs.gov or 1-800-TAX-FORM (1-800-829-3676). State tax forms can be obtained from the Federation of Tax Administrators at www.taxadmin.org.

It's a big job to close out anyone's earthly presence. If you're determined to file the person's final tax returns yourself, you're free to do so. But the learning curve can be steep. It's simpler and easier to delegate this responsibility to an accountant or other tax professional. It also costs money, but if the estate has the resources, that's usually the best way to go—and the larger the estate, the more prudent this becomes.

If You Want a Grave Marker, Purchase and Place It

There's no rush, but after the dust has settled, you should consider a grave marker, especially if the person specified one in the will or if there's a family plot. Most grave markers are simple, with just the person's name and dates of birth and death. But they can also contain quotations or imagery. In many communities, monument makers are located near cemeteries. If not, they're easy to find in the Yellow Pages or on the Internet. The simplest marker is a "flat," an engraved stone that sits almost flush with the ground. Flats start at around $300. Classic tombstones, "uprights," start at around $1,000. Or you might prefer a bronze marker. They start at around $300.

Since many people are no longer buried in a cemetery, other types of memorial markers are available. Many public places allow for the placement of plaques or markers if the person frequented the park or facility. Placing a bench with a plaque or planting a tree in a public park (if permitted) in memory of the person is a wonderful tribute and provides a place for friends and family to gather for years to come.

Officially Terminate Your Role as Executor

The final task of settling an estate is to inform the IRS that the fiduciary relationship has ceased. The executor does this by filing another IRS form 56. The form is available from IRS offices or online at www.irs.gov/pub/irs-pdf/f56.pdf.

In addition, depending on the size and complexity of the estate, it might also be prudent to file two other IRS forms:

- Form 4810, Request for Prompt Assessment under Internal Revenue Code Section 6501(d)
- Form 5495, Request for Discharge from Personal Liability under Internal Revenue Code Section 2204 or 6905

Consult an accountant or estate attorney to determine if you should file these forms.

6

You're Done; Now Make Things Easy for Your Survivors

CHECKLIST

❑ Name an executor.

❑ Label your documents "My Estate Plan."

❑ Rent a safe-deposit box.

❑ If you have children under eighteen, arrange for their guardianship.

❑ If you have pets, arrange for their guardianship.

❏ Decide about organ donation.

❏ Write an advance directive for medical care (living will).

❏ Write a durable power of attorney for health care.

❏ Write your will.

❏ Consider legacy gifts.

❏ Ideally, reveal the terms of your will to your family and close friends.

❏ Add your executor as a cosigner on all your bank and investment accounts.

❏ Provide your executor with easy access to around $10,000 for funeral-related expenses.

❏ Consider joining a burial society.

❏ If you have requests for your funeral, state them.

❏ If you want to be buried, buy a grave site.

❏ If you want a grave marker or plaque, tell your executor and family.

❑ Place as many of your assets as possible into a living trust.

❑ Organize all documents relating to your assets and debts.

❑ Update your estate plan and asset and debt files regularly.

❑ If a professional prepares your income taxes, provide your executor's contact information.

❑ Consider giving gifts to your heirs and beneficiaries while you're still alive.

An old blues song says, "Everybody wants to go to heaven. Nobody wants to die." That's right, nobody wants to die, but the fact is, we all do. As you've learned, settling a loved one's affairs takes more time and effort than you think it should—even if the person did everything possible to make the process go smoothly. Unfortunately, many people don't plan well. A recent survey of more than 1,000 American adults shows that overall, only half have wills (71 percent of those over 50, but only 37 percent of those under 50), and a mere 40 percent have living wills that specify their wishes about end-of-life medical care (19 percent of 18-to-29-year-olds, 32 percent of those aged 30 to 49, 46 percent of 50-to-64-year-olds, and 67 percent of those 65 and older). In other words, one quarter to one third of people eligible for Social Security have no will or living will, which means that their end-of-life care may well cause family conflict, and settling their affairs is likely to be a burden on those they love. Is that what you want? If not, invest some time and money *now* to plan for the inevitable.

If you like, you can do much of the work on your own. Visit Nolo (www.nolo.com), *the* Web site for do-it-yourself legal work, and click on "Wills, Trusts, and Estate Planning" for books and other information on advance directives, medical powers of attorney, creating wills and trusts, and other elements of estate planning. If you do everything yourself, figure on spending a good deal of time (the equivalent of a few months) and about $150 out of pocket.

However, most people would rather consult an estate planning attorney. This saves a great deal of time and headache, and an attorney will know the quirks of the law in the state where you live. In a few hour-long consultations, most estate lawyers can draft all the documents that you and your survivors—especially your executor—need. As for cost, it varies based on the size and complexity of your estate, but for most people, advance directives, a medical power of attorney, a will, living trusts, and a comprehensive estate plan costs anywhere from several hundred dollars to a few thousand.

Name an Executor

Typically spouses choose each other as executors. If you're not married, select someone you trust—one of your children, another relative, or a close friend. Then choose a secondary executor in case your primary executor dies or becomes incapacitated. Identify your primary and secondary executors to your family and friends. Then write and sign a document naming your primary and secondary executors. Place this document in a desk drawer, file drawer, or box clearly marked "My Estate Plan." Also place a copy in a safe-deposit box.

Label Your Documents "My Estate Plan"

This is so easy, and it makes life much easier for your executor and family. Place copies of everything in a special file drawer or box—documents about your end-of-life care, organ donation, guardianship decisions, will, financial records, assets, and debts. Label it clearly so that grief-stricken survivors can easily identify it. In addition, share it—give copies to people such as your heirs and others you love and trust.

Rent a Safe-Deposit Box

Your house might burn down, taking all your records with it. Place copies of all the documents related to your end-of-life care and estate plan in a bank vault. Have your executor be a cosigner for the safe-deposit box, so that person has immediate access to its contents. Give your executor a key.

You can also store your will and other estate-plan documents online. At our Web site—WhenSomeoneDies.net—you can store copies of documents and specify who has access and when to give each person access.

If You Have Children under Eighteen, Arrange for Their Guardianship

In most states, legal guardianship extends until the youngest child is eighteen. Be sure your guardian is prepared to act as a stepparent for as long as necessary. Tell your family and close friends about your children's guardian. Write up the information on the guardian and add it to your estate-plan file drawer and safe-deposit box.

If you cannot decide on a guardian, then designate a few trusted individuals to make the decision for you. Note, however, that if the child is fourteen or older, most states allow the child to have input into guardianship decisions.

If You Have Pets, Arrange for Their Guardianship

Tell your family and close friends who has agreed to be your pet(s)'s guardian(s). Write it up and add it to your estate-plan file drawer and safe-deposit box. Also, allocate money in your will to the pet's guardian for the animal's care. That's better than leaving it to the pet because in many states, pets cannot inherit.

Decide about Organ Donation

Whatever you decide, tell your executor, family, and close friends. In addition, because motor vehicle fatalities are a major source of donated organs, if people choose to donate their organs, most states note this on drivers' licenses. Check with your state's department of motor vehicles. In addition, write up a document specifying your decision.

Write an Advance Directive for Medical Care (Living Will)

An advance directive, also known as a living will, specifies your wishes for end-of-life medical care. Typically, it says: "I do not want any extraordinary procedures used to prolong my life. I do not want to be kept alive in a vegetative state." In other words, an advance directive says: "When I'm ready to die, let me."

On the other hand, a living will may specify that you want to have your life extended as long as possible. It's up to you. Sign your advance directive and have it notarized. Give a copy to your executor and include it in your estate-plan file drawer and safe-deposit box.

Write a Durable Power of Attorney for Health Care

An advance directive states your wishes for end-of-life care and is usually legally binding on the family and medical personnel. But to make sure your wishes are legally enforced, include a durable power of attorney for health care. If you're incapacitated and cannot make your own medical decisions, this document authorizes someone else to make them for you. Most state bar associations have templates for durable power-of-attorney documents. We've also included a sample in the Appendix. Have your signature notarized. Give a copy to your executor, who is the person charged with enforcing it. Place one copy in your estate-plan file and another in your safe-deposit box.

Write Your Will

You *must* write a will. There are two ways to do this. A "holographic" will is one you write by hand and sign. Most states recognize the validity of holographic wills.

The other way is to use a typewritten or computer-generated document that complies with state law by carrying your signature and those of one or two witnesses.

Many state bar associations provide templates for wills. You can also find one at WhenSomeoneDies.net.

If you ever update your will, destroy your old will. The more old wills you have floating around, the more complicated things become for your executor.

Consider Legacy Gifts

I serve on the Board of the Sonoma Valley Fund in Sonoma, California. We are part of the Community Foundation of Sonoma County. Our purpose is to convince people to leave a portion of their estate to nonprofit, charitable organizations in their local communities. While charitable acts are deeply personal, and it is presumptuous of me or anyone to ask, please consider including one or more local charities in your will. The good that money will do after you are gone is immense, and your spirit will last for many years in the community you loved.

Ideally, Reveal the Terms of Your Will to Your Family and Close Friends

If everyone knows how you intend to distribute your estate before you die, this minimizes conflict after you're gone. However, if you plan to deliver any posthumous surprises, for example, disinheriting someone or making bequests you know will horrify your heirs, you may prefer to keep your will a secret. If your will contains anything unusual, it's best to inform your executor, so that person can anticipate any conflict and perhaps take steps to minimize it. But you don't have to. Your will is entirely up to you, and so is how you decide to reveal its contents.

Add Your Executor as a Cosigner on All Your Bank and Investment Accounts

This makes your assets immediately available to pay for your funeral and other expenses, for example, airfare for loved ones who could not otherwise afford to attend your funeral, or shipping your pet to a distant guardian. Having a cosigner also means that the funds are available during any probate and are easily and quickly available to your heirs.

Provide Your Executor with Easy Access to around $10,000 for Funeral-Related Expenses

Depending on your circumstances, this may or may not be possible, but if it is, it's virtually certain to save your executor and your family time and heartache. Funerals and burials may not cost as much as $10,000 but it never hurts to have funds available to do things such as changing the locks on your home, hiring a gardener to maintain the grounds, and contracting for home repairs to prepare your home for sale.

Consider Joining a Burial Society

Membership usually means funeral and burial cost savings. Add the documents to your estate-plan file, and tell your executor, family, and close friends.

If You Have Requests for Your Funeral, State Them

What type of funeral do you want? Is there anyone you'd like to officiate? Do you want to be buried or cremated? Do you want your remains prepared in a "green" way? Do you want a less formal memorial instead of a traditional funeral? Do you want a memorial at some point after your funeral? If these issues are important to you, include your wishes in your will, or file the document in your estate-plan file, store it in your safe-deposit box, and tell your executor, family, and close friends.

If You Want to Be Buried,
Buy a Grave Site

Add the deed to your estate-plan file and place a copy in your safe-deposit box. Inform your executor and your family of the location of your grave site. You might also consider buying several grave sites adjacent to one another to create a family plot.

If You Want a Grave Marker or Plaque,
Tell Your Executor and Family

If you know what you'd like your marker to say, write it down, and add that information to your estate-plan file and safe-deposit box.

Place as Many of Your Assets
as Possible into a Living Trust

You may know people with "trust funds." But few people understand what trusts are and how they work as part of a comprehensive estate plan. If you or you and your spouse own assets, particularly a home, other real estate, and investment securities, it's prudent to place these assets into a trust known as a "living," "spousal," or "A/B trust."

Why create a trust? Because the assets it holds do not go through probate. They pass immediately to your heirs and beneficiaries—no lawyers, courts, or judges are involved. While you live, you (or you and your spouse) should be the trustee (or co-trustees). Upon your death (or after the death of both spouses), someone you designate becomes the trustee.

But setting up a trust may feel disconcerting. As soon as you place your assets in the trust, technically you no longer own them. The trust does. The trust is not exactly a separate legal entity (as a corporation would be), but legally it's treated like one. However, you control the trust, so you continue to control the assets in the trust; for all practical purposes, you still own your assets. But for purposes of estate planning, the trust makes distribution of your assets much easier for your executor and much faster and less complicated for your heirs and beneficiaries.

For example, John and Mary Smith assign all their property to the "John and Mary Smith Living Trust." After the property goes into the trust, John and Mary become the trustees. As co-trustees, technically, they no longer "own" the property, but they control the trust's assets and can do whatever they want with them. When they form the trust, they also name beneficiaries, the people or organizations that will inherit the trust's assets when John and Mary die. In most spousal trusts, John and Mary designate their children as the beneficiaries. If they have no children, they designate someone else.

While John and Mary are alive, for all practical purposes

their trust is irrelevant. They continue to enjoy their money, property, and other assets. However, the title to any property changes. The title no longer says "owned by John and Mary Smith." Now the title specifies "John and Mary Smith, as trustees of the John and Mary Smith Living Trust." If John and Mary sell the property, they sign the paperwork not as the owners but as their trust's trustees. But it's still their property.

When one of them dies, the question becomes: Who is the successor trustee? To answer that, we need to find the document that created the trust in the first place. Typically, it is titled "The John and Mary Smith Living Trust Established on [insert date]." In the first few pages, there is a paragraph titled something like "Original Trustees and Successor Trustees." That paragraph tells you who is (are) the trustee (co-trustees), and if one dies (or both), who can become the successor trustee.

Whoever the successor trustee is, that person must complete a simple affidavit that officially identifies the new trustee, and provide the affidavit and a death certificate to every institution that holds trust assets.

What happens after both John and Mary die? Usually, the successor trustee (one of their children, another relative or a friend, or sometimes their lawyer) dissolves the trust and distributes the assets. This is very simple. The trustee fills out the necessary forms, which may require you to supply a copy of the trust, a death certificate for the last-to-die spouse, and instructions for new title.

But before the successor trustee distributes the trust's assets, all of the deceased's bills, expenses, and taxes must be paid—and the trust must also file a tax return and pay any taxes on its income (see Chapter 5).

Organize All Documents
Relating to Your Assets and Debts

Asset documents include statements from banks, investment accounts, or pensions—proof of any source of income. Debt documents include mortgages, car loans, other loans, and information about any money you owe anyone. Place these in your estate-plan file. Place copies in your safe-deposit box.

Update Your Estate Plan and Asset
and Debt Files Regularly

If your personal situation changes—you get divorced, your children become adults, and so on—revise your will.

Investment firms typically issue quarterly statements. Throw away the previous statements in your estate-plan file and add the new ones. Make copies and add them to your safe-deposit box, throwing away the old ones. Ideally, do this quarterly, but annually is sufficient. The important thing is to have all your recent financial records, what you own and what you owe, collected in two convenient places, your estate-plan file and your safe-deposit box. This makes things as easy as possible for your executor and your family.

If a Professional Prepares Your Income Taxes, Provide Your Executor's Contact Information

Your executor is responsible for your taxes and the taxes of any trust and should have easy access to your tax preparer, and vice versa.

Consider Giving Gifts to Your Heirs and Beneficiaries While You're Still Alive

Why wait until you're dead to help your loved ones with college tuition, home purchases, and other substantial expenses? As this book goes to press, annual gifts to any one person of up to $13,000 are tax-free—the gift giver (you) can't deduct the gift amount from taxes and the recipient is not obligated to report the gift as income and pay taxes on it. The maximum amount for tax-free gifts changes, so if you're interested in giving substantial gifts, consult an accountant or estate lawyer.

If you'd like to help young loved ones by contributing to their college expenses, consider creating a 529 plan, named for Section 529 of the Internal Revenue Code, which created this option in 1996. Under a 529 plan, you deposit cash or securities in an account at a bank or brokerage firm in the name of the relative you wish to help. As the donor, you control the 529 account and decide when to withdraw money. If the child decides not to attend college, you can cancel the plan and reclaim your contributions. Every state now has 529 options, and in most states, it doesn't matter where the student attends college. Your contributions are not deductible, but your investment grows tax-deferred, and is ultimately federally tax-free. Your state may offer tax benefits for educational expenses equivalent to 529 plans as well. Check with an accountant or tax person.

If you're affluent, you might also set up trusts for your children, grandchildren, and others. Consult an estate attorney.

Further Resources

WEB SITES

AMERICAN SOCIETY OF APPRAISERS

http://www.appraisers.org
Find an appraiser near you to determine the value of bequeathed art, jewelry, collectibles, businesses, and so on.

CARING.COM

http://www.caring.com
A resource for caregivers. Includes a broadcast feature to notify friends and family of a loved one's ailing health or passing.

DEPARTMENT OF VETERANS AFFAIRS BURIAL AND MEMORIAL BENEFITS

http://www.cem.va.gov
Visit to secure burial flags, schedule a burial, and learn more about national cemeteries in your area.

FACEBOOK DEACTIVATION

**http://www.facebook.com/help/contact.php?show_
form=deceased**
Deactivate or memorialize a loved one's Facebook account.

FEDERAL OFFICE OF PERSONNEL MANAGEMENT

http://www.opm.gov
Survivors of federal employees and former federal employees can learn more about their eligibility for benefits.

FEDERAL TRADE COMMISSION

http://ftc.gov/bcp/menus/consumer/shop/funeral.shtm
Contains "Funerals: A Consumer Guide" and articles outlining your rights as a consumer and considerations when choosing a funeral home.

FEDERATION OF TAX ADMINISTRATORS

http://www.taxadmin.org
All state tax forms are available here.

FUNERAL CONSUMER GUARDIAN SOCIETY

http://www.funeralconsumer.org
Contains a funeral cost estimator.

INTERNAL REVENUE SERVICE

http://www.irs.gov
Visit to download federal tax forms or obtain an EIN number to pay taxes on an estate. For IRS Form 56, "Notice Concerning Fiduciary Relationship," go to www.irs.gov/pub/irs-pdf/f56.pdf

NOLO

http://www.nolo.com
A resource for do-it-yourself legal work. Click on "Wills, Trusts, and Estate Planning" for books and other information on advance directives, medical powers of attorney, creating wills and trusts, and other elements of estate planning.

Obituary Guide

http://obituaryguide.com/template.php
A free obituary template to help you craft the perfect biographical account.

Parents of Murdered Children

http://www.pomc.com
An online extension of the nationwide organization.

Probate Law Resources

Laws in every state specify estate values that trigger probate proceedings. Find out more at these Web sites:

Findlaw Estate Planning, at http://estate.findlaw.com
Estate Settlement.com, at http://www.estatesettlement.com
Estate Finance, at http://www.estatefinance.com

Survivors of Suicide

http://www.survivorsofsuicide.com
An interactive forum and support group.

Useful Telephone Numbers

FEDERAL OFFICE OF PERSONNEL MANAGEMENT

1-888-767-6738

Survivors of federal employees and former federal employees can learn more about their eligibility for benefits.

INTERNAL REVENUE SERVICE

1-800-829-4933; 1-800-TAX-FORM (1-800-829-3676)

SOCIAL SECURITY ADMINISTRATION

1 800-772-1213

You are obligated to report a death to Social Security by phone. At the time of writing, deaths cannot be reported online.

VETERANS ADMINISTRATION

1-800-827-1000

Call to inquire about benefits for surviving spouses.

Appendix

SAMPLE LEGAL FORMS
AND A MODEL OBITUARY

Legal forms are often intimidating. We've included samples in the hope that they help you feel more comfortable with the documents you must deal with as an executor and the documents you create for your own estate planning. Laws affecting documents such as medical powers of attorney vary from state to state, so you may need an attorney to customize them for your own situation, but these California forms are a good place to begin the process.

This form can be used to document your "end of life" medical directions. Do you want invasive surgery? Life support? It also allows you to make organ donations and provide your primary doctor's acknowledgment that he reviewed your choices with you. It is important that you also give someone the "power of attorney" to ensure the doctors and the hospital follow your directions.

SAMPLE ADVANCE HEALTH CARE DIRECTIVE

Explanation

You have the right to give instructions about your own health care. You also have the right to name someone else to make health care decisions for you. This form lets you do either or both of these things. It also lets you express your wishes regarding donation of organs and the designation of your primary physician. If you use this form, you may complete or modify all or any part of it. You are free to use a different form.

Part 1 of this form is a power of attorney for health care. Part 1 lets you name another individual as agent to make health care decisions for you if you become incapable of making your own decisions or if you want someone else to make those decisions for you now even though you are still capable. You may also name an alternate agent to act for you if your first choice is not willing, able, or reasonably available to make decisions for you. (Your agent may not be an operator or employee of a community care facility or a residential care facility where you are receiving care, or your supervising health care provider or employee of the health care institution where you are receiving care, unless your agent is related to you or is a coworker.)

Unless the form you sign limits the authority of your agent, your agent may make all health care decisions for you. This form has a place for you to limit the authority of your agent. You need not limit the authority of your agent if you wish to rely on your agent for all health care decisions that may have to be made. If you choose not to limit the authority of your agent, your agent will have the right to:

(a) Consent or refuse consent to any care, treatment, service, or procedure to maintain, diagnose, or otherwise affect a physical or mental condition.

(b) Select or discharge health care providers and institutions.

(c) Approve or disapprove diagnostic tests, surgical procedures, and programs of medication.

(d) Direct the provision, withholding, or withdrawal of artificial nutrition and hydration and all other forms of health care, including cardiopulmonary resuscitation.

(e) Make anatomical gifts, authorize an autopsy, and direct disposition of remains.

Part 2 of this form lets you give specific instructions about any aspect of your health care, whether or not you appoint an agent. Choices are provided for you to express your wishes regarding the provision, withholding, or withdrawal of treatment to keep you alive, as well as the provision of pain relief. Space is also provided for you to add to the choices you have made or for you to write out any additional wishes. If you are satisfied to allow your agent to determine what is best for you in making end-of-life decisions, you need not fill out Part 2 of this form.

Part 3 of this form lets you express an intention to donate your bodily organs and tissues following your death.

Part 4 of this form lets you designate a physician to have primary responsibility for your health care.

After completing this form, sign and date the form at the end. The form must be signed by two qualified witnesses or acknowledged before a notary public. Give a copy of the signed and completed form to your physician, to any other health care providers you may have, to any health care institution at which you are receiving care, and to any health care agents you have named. You should talk to the person you have named as agent to make sure that he or she understands your wishes and is willing to take the responsibility.

You have the right to revoke this advance health care directive or replace this form at any time.

PART 1:
POWER OF ATTORNEY FOR HEALTH CARE

1.1 DESIGNATION OF AGENT: I designate the following individual as my agent to make health care decisions for me:

I, _____, do hereby designate and appoint

_____

_____

_____

PH: _____

OPTIONAL: If I revoke my agent's authority or if my agent is not willing, able, or reasonably available to make a health care decision for me, I designate as my first alternate agent:

_____

(name of individual you choose as first alternate agent)

_____

(address)   *(city)*   *(state)*   *(zip code)*

_____

(home phone)   *(work phone)*

OPTIONAL: If I revoke the authority of my agent and first alternate agent or if neither is willing, able, or reasonably available to make a health care decision for me, I designate as my second alternate agent:

_____

(name of individual you choose as second alternate agent)

_____

(address)   *(city)*   *(state)*   *(zip code)*

(home phone)   _(work phone)_

1.2 AGENT'S AUTHORITY: My agent is authorized to make all health care decisions for me, including decisions to provide, withhold, or withdraw artificial nutrition and hydration and all other forms of health care to keep me alive, except as I state here:

HIPAA Release Authority. I intend for my agent to be treated as I would be with respect to my rights regarding the use and disclosure of my individually identifiable health information or other medical records. This release authority applies to any information governed by the Health Insurance Portability and Accountability Act of 1996 (aka HIPAA), 42 U.S.C. 1320d and 45 C.F.R. 160-164. I authorize any physician, health care professional, dentist, health plan, hospital, clinic, laboratory, pharmacy, or other covered health care provider, any insurance company and the Medical Information Bureau Inc. or other health care clearinghouse that has provided treatment or services to me, or that has paid for or is seeking payment from me for such services, to give, disclose and release to my agent, without restriction, all of my individually identifiable health information and medical records regarding any past, present, or future medical or mental health condition. The authority given my agent shall supersede any prior agreement that I may have made with my health care providers to restrict access to or disclosure of my individually identifiable health information. The authority given my agent has no expiration date and shall expire only in the event that I revoke the authority in writing and deliver it to my health care provider.

1.3 WHEN AGENT'S AUTHORITY BECOMES EFFEC-TIVE: My agent's authority becomes effective when my primary physician determines that I am unable to make my own health care decisions unless I mark the following box.

If I mark this box ❑, my agent's authority to make health care decisions for me takes effect immediately.

1.4 AGENT'S OBLIGATION: My agent shall make health care decisions for me in accordance with this power of attorney for health care, any instructions I give in Part 2 of this form, and my other wishes to the extent known to my agent. To the extent my wishes are unknown, my agent shall make health care decisions for me in accordance with what my agent determines to be in my best interest. In determining my best interest, my agent shall consider my personal values to the extent known to my agent.

1.5 AGENT'S POSTDEATH AUTHORITY: My agent is authorized to make anatomical gifts, authorize an autopsy, and direct disposition of my remains, except as I state here or in Part 3 of this form:

_____

_____

(Add additional sheets if needed.)

1.6 NOMINATION OF CONSERVATOR: If a conservator of my person needs to be appointed for me by a court, I nominate the agent designated in this form. If that agent is not willing, able, or reasonably available to act as conservator, I nominate the alternate agents whom I have named, in the order designated.

PART 2: INSTRUCTIONS FOR HEALTH CARE

If you fill out this Part of the form, you may strike any wording you do not want.

2.1 END-OF-LIFE DECISIONS: I direct that my health care providers and others involved in my care provide, withhold, or withdraw treatment in accordance with the choice I have marked below:

❑ (a) Choice Not to Prolong Life

I do not want my life to be prolonged if (1) I have an incurable and irreversible condition that will result in my death within a relatively short time, (2) I become unconscious and, to a reasonable degree of medical certainty, I will not regain consciousness, or (3) the likely risks and burdens of treatment would outweigh the expected benefits, **OR**

❑ (b) Choice to Prolong Life

I want my life to be prolonged as long as possible within the limits of generally accepted health care standards.

2.2 RELIEF FROM PAIN: Except as I state in the following space, I direct that treatment for alleviation of pain or discomfort be provided at all times, even if it hastens my death:

_____

_____

(Add additional sheets if needed.)

2.3 OTHER WISHES: (If you do not agree with any of the optional choices above and wish to write your own, or if you wish to add to the instructions you have given above, you may do so here.) I direct that:

_____

_____

(Add additional sheets if needed.)

PART 3:
DONATION OF ORGANS AT DEATH (OPTIONAL)

3.1 Upon my death (mark applicable box):

    ❏ (a) I give any needed organs, tissues, or parts, **OR**

    ❏ (b) I give the following organs, tissues, or parts only:_____.

❏ (c) My gift is for the following purposes (strike any of the following you do not want):

(1) Transplant

(2) Therapy

(3) Research

(4) Education

PART 4: PRIMARY PHYSICIAN (OPTIONAL)

4.1 I designate the following physician as my primary physician:

_____

(name of physician)

_____

(address)   *(city)*   *(state)*   *(zip code)*

_____

(home phone)   *(work phone)*

OPTIONAL: If the physician I have designated above is not willing, able, or reasonably available to act as my primary physician, I designate the following physician as my primary physician:

_____

(name of physician)

_____

(address)   (city)   (state)   (zip code)

_____

(home phone)   (work phone)

PART 5:

5.1 EFFECT OF COPY: A copy of this form has the same effect as the original.

5.2 SIGNATURE: Sign and date the form here:

_____

Date: _____

5.3 STATEMENT OF WITNESSES: I declare under penalty of perjury under the laws of California (1) that the individual who signed or acknowledged this advance health care directive is personally known to me, or that the individual's identity was proven to me by convincing evidence, (2) that the individual signed or acknowledged this advance directive in my presence, (3) that the individual appears to be of sound mind and under no duress, fraud, or undue influence, (4) that I am not a person appointed as agent by this advance directive, and (5) that I am not the individual's health care provider, an employee of the individual's health care provider, the operator of a community care facility, an employee of an operator of a community care facility, the operator of a residential care facility for the elderly, nor an employee of an operator of a residential care facility for the elderly.

First witness: **Second witness:**

_____   _____
(print name)   *(print name)*

_____   _____
(address)   *(address)*

_____   _____
(city)   *(state)*   *(city)*   *(state)*

_____   _____
(signature of witness)   *(signature of witness)*

_____   _____
(date)   *(date)*

5.4 ADDITIONAL STATEMENT OF WITNESSES: At least one of the above witnesses must also sign the following declaration:

I further declare under penalty of perjury under the laws of California that I am not related to the individual executing this advance health care directive by blood, marriage, or adoption, and to the best of my knowledge, I am not entitled to any part of the individual's estate upon his or her death under a will now existing or by operation of law.

_____   _____
(signature of witness)   *(signature of witness)*

PART 6: SPECIAL WITNESS REQUIREMENT

6.1 The following statement is required only if you are a patient in a skilled nursing facility—a health care facility that provides the following basic services: skilled nursing care and supportive care to patients whose primary need is for availability of skilled nursing care on an extended basis. The patient advocate or ombudsman must sign the following statement:

STATEMENT OF PATIENT ADVOCATE OR OMBUDSMAN

I declare under penalty of perjury under the laws of California that I am a patient advocate or ombudsman as designated by the State Department of Aging and that I am serving as a witness as required by Section 4675 of the Probate Code.

_____   _____
(date)   *(sign your name)*

_____	_____
(address)	*(print your name)*
_____	_____
(city) *(state)*	*(Social Security number)*

STATE OF CALIFORNIA

COUNTY OF _____

On_____, 2012, before me,_____, Notary Public, personally appeared _____, who proved to me on the basis of satisfactory evidence to be the person whose name is subscribed to the within instrument, and acknowledged to me that he/she executed the same in his/her authorized capacity, and that by his/her signatures on the instrument the person, or the entity upon behalf of which the person acted, executed the instrument.

I certify under PENALTY OF PERJURY under the laws of the State of California that the foregoing paragraph is true and correct.

WITNESS my hand and official seal.

(Seal)

Notary Public

This form can be used to give someone the "power of attorney" to make financial and business decisions if you become mentally incapacitated. Most people give their power of attorney to their spouse, their brother or sister, or an older child.

SAMPLE UNIFORM STATUTORY FORM
POWER OF ATTORNEY

NOTICE: THE POWERS GRANTED BY THIS DOC-
UMENT ARE BROAD AND SWEEPING. THEY ARE
EXPLAINED IN THE UNIFORM STATUTORY FORM
POWER OF ATTORNEY ACT (CALIFORNIA PROBATE
CODE SECTIONS 4400-4465, INCLUSIVE). IF YOU HAVE
ANY QUESTIONS ABOUT THESE POWERS, OBTAIN
COMPETENT LEGAL ADVICE. THIS DOCUMENT DOES
NOT AUTHORIZE ANYONE TO MAKE MEDICAL AND
OTHER HEALTH CARE DECISIONS FOR YOU. YOU MAY
REVOKE THIS POWER OF ATTORNEY IF YOU LATER
WISH TO DO SO.

I,_____ , appoint

_____

_____

_____

as my agent (attorney-in-fact) to act for me in any lawful
way with respect to the following initialed subjects:

TO GRANT ALL OF THE FOLLOWING POWERS, INI-
TIAL THE LINE IN FRONT OF (N) AND IGNORE THE
LINES IN FRONT OF THE OTHER POWERS.

TO GRANT ONE OR MORE, BUT FEWER THAN ALL, OF THE FOLLOWING POWERS, INITIAL THE LINE IN FRONT OF EACH POWER YOU ARE GRANTING.

TO WITHHOLD A POWER, DO NOT INITIAL THE LINE IN FRONT OF IT. YOU MAY, BUT NEED NOT, CROSS OUT EACH POWER WITHHELD.

INITIAL:

_____   (A)   Real property transactions.

_____   (B)   Tangible personal property transactions.

_____   (C)   Stock and bond transactions.

_____   (D)   Commodity and option transactions.

_____   (E)   Banking and other financial institution transactions.

_____   (F)   Business operating transactions.

_____   (G)   Insurance and annuity transactions.

_____   (H)   Estate, trust, and other beneficiary transactions.

_____   (I)   Claims and litigation.

_____   (J)   Personal and family maintenance.

_____   (K)   Benefits from Social Security, Medicare, Medicaid, or other governmental programs, or civil or military service.

_____   (L)   Retirement plan transactions.

_____ (M) Tax matters.

_____ (N) ALL OF THE POWERS LISTED ABOVE.

YOU NEED NOT INITIAL ANY OTHER LINES IF YOU INITIAL LINE (N).

SPECIAL INSTRUCTIONS:

ON THE FOLLOWING LINES YOU MAY GIVE SPECIAL INSTRUCTIONS LIMITING OR EXTENDING THE POWERS GRANTED TO YOUR AGENT.

The grant of the foregoing powers shall only take effect and is specifically conditioned upon the determination by at least two (2) licensed medical physicians (evidenced by written declarations under penalty of perjury) that I am incompetent and unable to manage my affairs.

The powers granted above include the power to make gifts or charitable contributions of my property on my behalf for income tax and estate planning purposes to my relatives or to those beneficiaries of my Will or of any funded revocable trust of which I am the grantor, and to withdraw assets of any such revocable trust on my behalf in order to accomplish such gifts or contributions. Such authority is specifically limited to gifts which qualify for the federal annual exclusion from the gift tax under Section 2503(b) of the Internal Revenue Code of 1986, as amended, and which do not satisfy any legal support obligation of my agent.

UNLESS YOU DIRECT OTHERWISE ABOVE, THIS POWER OF ATTORNEY IS EFFECTIVE IMMEDIATELY AND WILL CONTINUE UNTIL IT IS REVOKED.

This power of attorney will continue to be effective even though I become incapacitated.

STRIKE THE PRECEDING SENTENCE IF YOU DO NOT WANT THIS POWER OF ATTORNEY TO CONTINUE IF YOU BECOME INCAPACITATED.

EXERCISE OF POWER OF ATTORNEY WHERE MORE THAN ONE AGENT IS DESIGNATED

If I have designated more than one agent, the agents are to act _____.

IF YOU APPOINTED MORE THAN ONE AGENT AND YOU WANT EACH AGENT TO BE ABLE TO ACT ALONE WITHOUT THE OTHER AGENT JOINING, WRITE THE WORD "SEPARATELY" IN THE BLANK SPACE ABOVE. IF YOU DO NOT INSERT ANY WORD IN THE BLANK SPACE, OR IF YOU INSERT THE WORD "JOINTLY," THEN ALL OF YOUR AGENTS MUST ACT OR SIGN TOGETHER.

I agree that any third party who receives a copy of this document may act under it. Revocation of the power of attorney is not effective as to a third party until the third party has actual knowledge of the revocation. I agree to indemnify the third party for any claims that arise against the third party because of reliance on this power of attorney.

Signed this _____ day of _____, 2012.

_____

Social Security No._____

State of California

County of _____

BY ACCEPTING OR ACTING UNDER THE APPOINT-MENT, THE AGENT ASSUMES THE FIDUCIARY AND OTHER LEGAL RESPONSIBILITIES OF AN AGENT.

CERTIFICATE OF ACKNOWLEDGMENT
OF NOTARY PUBLIC

STATE OF CALIFORNIA

COUNTY OF _____

Social Security Number: _____

On_____, 2012, before me,
_____, Notary Public, personally
appeared _____, who proved to me on
the basis of satisfactory evidence to be the person whose name
is subscribed to the within instrument and acknowledged to me
that he/she executed the same in his/her authorized capacity,
and that by his/her signature on the instrument the person, or
the entity upon behalf of which the person acted, executed the
instrument.

I certify under PENALTY OF PERJURY under the laws of
the State of California that the foregoing paragraph is true and
correct.

WITNESS my hand and official seal.

_____

Notary Public   *(Seal)*

[this page left blank]

This is California's "statutory will." It is made available so that people can write a valid will without a lawyer. Most states have similar forms. Check the Web site for your state's attorney ("Bar") association.

CALIFORNIA STATUTORY WILL

QUESTIONS AND ANSWERS ABOUT THIS CALIFORNIA STATUTORY WILL

The following information, in question and answer form, is not a part of the California Statutory Will. It is designed to help you understand about Wills and to decide if this Will meets your needs. This Will is in a simple form. The complete text of each paragraph of this Will is printed at the end of the Will.

1. What happens if I die without a Will? If you die without a Will, what you own (your "assets") in your name alone will be divided among your spouse, children, or other relatives according to state law. The court will appoint a relative to collect and distribute your assets.

2. What can a Will do for me? In a Will you may designate who will receive your assets at your death. You may designate someone (called an "executor") to appear before the court, collect your assets, pay your debts and taxes, and distribute your assets as you specify. You may nominate someone (called a "guardian") to raise your children who are under age 18. You may designate someone (called a "custodian") to manage assets for your children until they reach any age between 18 and 25.

3. Does a Will avoid probate? No. With or without a Will, assets in your name alone usually go through the court probate process. The court's first job is to determine if your Will is valid.

4. What is community property? Can I give away my share in my Will? If you are married and you or your spouse earned money during your marriage from work and wages, that money (and the assets bought with it) is community property. Your Will can only give away your one-half of community property. Your Will cannot give away your spouse's one-half of community property.

5. Does my Will give away all of my assets? Do all assets go through probate? No. Money in a joint tenancy bank account automatically belongs to the other named owner without probate. If your spouse or child is on the deed to your house as a joint tenant, the house automatically passes to him or her. Life insurance and retirement plan benefits may pass directly to the named beneficiary. A Will does not necessarily control how these types of "nonprobate" assets pass at your death.

6. Are there different kinds of Wills? Yes. There are handwritten Wills, typewritten Wills, attorney-prepared Wills, and statutory Wills. All are valid if done precisely as the law requires. You should see a lawyer if you do not want to use this statutory Will or if you do not understand this form.

7. Who may use this Will? This Will is based on California law. It is designed only for California residents. You may use this form if you are single, married, or divorced. You must be age 18 or older and of sound mind.

8. Are there any reasons why I should NOT use this statutory Will? Yes. This is a simple Will. It is not designed to reduce

death taxes or other taxes. Talk to a lawyer to do tax planning, especially if (i) your assets will be worth more than $600,000 at your death, (ii) you own business-related assets, (iii) you want to create a trust fund for your children's education or other purposes, (iv) you own assets in some other state, (v) you want to disinherit your spouse or descendants, or (vi) you have valuable interests in pension or profit sharing plans. You should talk to a lawyer who knows about estate planning if this Will does not meet your needs. This Will treats most adopted children like natural children. You should talk to a lawyer if you have stepchildren or foster children whom you have not adopted.

9. May I add or cross out any words on this Will? No. If you do, the Will may be invalid or the court may ignore the crossed out or added words. You may only fill in the blanks. You may amend this Will by a separate document (called a codicil). Talk to a lawyer if you want to do something with your assets which is not allowed in this form.

10. May I change my Will? Yes. A Will is not effective until you die. You may make and sign a new Will. You may change your Will at any time, but only by an amendment (called a codicil). You can give away or sell your assets before your death. Your Will only acts on what you own at death.

11. Where should I keep my Will? After you and the witness sign the Will, keep your Will in your safe-deposit box or other safe place. You should tell trusted family members where your Will is kept.

12. When should I change my Will? You should make and sign a new Will if you marry or divorce after you sign this Will. Divorce or annulment automatically cancels all property stated to pass to a former husband or wife under this Will, and revokes the designation of a former spouse as executor, custodian, or guardian. You should sign a new Will when you have more children, or if your spouse or a child dies. You may want to change your Will if there is a large change in the value of your assets.

13. What can I do if I do not understand something in this Will? If there is anything in this Will you do not understand, ask a lawyer to explain it to you.

14. What is an executor? An "executor" is the person you name to collect your assets, pay your debts and taxes, and distribute your assets as the court directs. It may be a person or it may be a qualified bank or trust company.

15. Should I require a bond? You may require that an executor post a "bond." A bond is a form of insurance to replace assets that may be mismanaged or stolen by the executor. The cost of the bond is paid from the estate's assets.

16. What is a guardian? Do I need to designate one? If you have children under age 18, you should designate a guardian of their "persons" to raise them.

17. What is a custodian? Do I need to designate one? A "custodian" is a person you may designate to manage assets for someone (including a child) who is between ages 18 and 25 and

who receives assets under your Will. The custodian manages the assets and pays as much as the custodian determines is proper for health, support, maintenance, and education. The custodian delivers what is left to the person when the person reaches the age you choose (between 18 and 25). No bond is required of a custodian.

18. Should I ask people if they are willing to serve before I designate them as executor, guardian, or custodian? Probably yes. Some people and banks and trust companies may not consent to serve or may not be qualified to act.

19. What happens if I make a gift in this Will to someone and they die before I do? A person must survive you by 120 hours to take a gift under this Will. If they do not, then the gift fails and goes with the rest of your assets. If the person who does not survive you is a relative of you or your spouse, then certain assets may go to the relative's descendants.

20. What is a trust? There are many kinds of trusts, including trusts created by Wills (called "testamentary trusts") and trusts created during your lifetime (called "revocable living trusts"). Both kinds of trusts are long-term arrangements where a manager (called a "trustee") invests and manages assets for someone (called a "beneficiary") on the terms you specify. Trusts are too complicated to be used in this statutory Will. You should see a lawyer if you want to create a trust.

INSTRUCTIONS

1. READ THE WILL. Read the whole Will first. If you do not understand something, ask a lawyer to explain it to you.

2. FILL IN THE BLANKS. Fill in the blanks. Follow the instructions in the form carefully. Do not add any words to the Will (except for filling in blanks) or cross out any words.

3. DATE AND SIGN THE WILL AND HAVE TWO WITNESSES SIGN IT. Date and sign the Will and have two witnesses sign it. You and the witnesses should read and follow the Notice to Witnesses found at the end of this Will.

CALIFORNIA STATUTORY WILL OF

Print Your Full Name:

_____

1. Will. This is my Will. I revoke all prior Wills and codicils.

2. Specific Gift of Personal Residence. (Optional—use only if you want to give your personal residence to a different person or persons than you give the balance of your assets to under paragraph 5 below.) I give my interest in my principal personal residence at the time of my death (subject to mortgages and liens) as follows (select one choice only and sign in the box after your choice):

Choice One: All to my spouse, if my spouse survives me; otherwise to my descendants (my children and the descendants of my children) who survive me.

```
┌─────────────────────────────────────────────────────┐
│                                                     │
└─────────────────────────────────────────────────────┘
```

Choice Two: Nothing to my spouse; all to my descendants (my children and the descendants of my children) who survive me.

```
┌─────────────────────────────────────────────────────┐
│                                                     │
└─────────────────────────────────────────────────────┘
```

Choice Three: All to the following person if he or she survives me (insert the name of the person):

_____

```
┌─────────────────────────────────────────────────────┐
│                                                     │
└─────────────────────────────────────────────────────┘
```

Choice Four: Equally among the following persons who survive me (insert the names of two or more persons):

_____

_____

_____

```
┌─────────────────────────────────────────────────────┐
│                                                     │
└─────────────────────────────────────────────────────┘
```

3. Specific Gift of Automobiles, Household and Personal Effects. (Optional—use only if you want to give automobiles and household and personal effects to a different person or persons than you give the balance of your assets to under paragraph 5 below.) I give all of my automobiles (subject to loans), furniture, furnishings, household items, clothing, jewelry, and other tangible articles of a personal nature at the time of my death as follows (select one choice only and sign in the box after your choice):

Choice One: All to my spouse, if my spouse survives me; otherwise to my descendants (my children and the descendants of my children) who survive me.

```
┌─────────────────────────────────────────────────────┐
│                                                     │
└─────────────────────────────────────────────────────┘
```

Choice Two: Nothing to my spouse; all to my descendants (my children and the descendants of my children) who survive me.

```
┌─────────────────────────────────────────────────────┐
│                                                     │
└─────────────────────────────────────────────────────┘
```

Choice Three: All to the following person if he or she survives me (insert the name of the person):

_____

```
┌─────────────────────────────────────────────────────┐
│                                                     │
└─────────────────────────────────────────────────────┘
```

Choice Four: Equally among the following persons who survive me (insert the names of two or more persons):

_____

_____

_____

_____

```
┌─────────────────────────────────────────┐
│                                         │
└─────────────────────────────────────────┘
```

4. Specific Gifts of Cash. (Optional) I make the following cash gifts to the persons named below who survive me, or to the named charity, and I sign my name in the box after each gift. If I don't sign in the box, I do not make a gift. (Sign in the box after each gift you make.)

Name of Person or Charity to receive gift (Name one only—please print) Amount of Cash Gift

```
┌─────────────────────────────────────────┐
│                                         │
└─────────────────────────────────────────┘
```
Sign your name in the box to make this gift

Name of Person or Charity to receive gift (Name one only—please print) Amount of Cash Gift

```
┌─────────────────────────────────────────┐
│                                         │
└─────────────────────────────────────────┘
```
Sign your name in the box to make this gift

Name of Person or Charity to receive gift (Name one only—please print) Amount of Cash Gift

```
┌─────────────────────────────────────────┐
│                                         │
└─────────────────────────────────────────┘
```
Sign your name in the box to make this gift

Name of Person or Charity to receive gift (Name one only—please print) Amount of Cash Gift

```
┌─────────────────────────────────────────────────┐
│                                                 │
└─────────────────────────────────────────────────┘
```

Sign your name in the box to make this gift

Name of Person or Charity to receive gift (Name one only—please print) Amount of Cash Gift

```
┌─────────────────────────────────────────────────┐
│                                                 │
└─────────────────────────────────────────────────┘
```

Sign your name in the box to make this gift

5. Balance of My Assets. Except for the specific gifts made in paragraphs 2, 3, and 4 above, I give the balance of my assets as follows (Select one choice only and sign in the box after your choice. If you sign in more than one box or if you don't sign in any box, the court will distribute your assets as if you did not make a Will.):

Choice One: All to my spouse, if my spouse survives me; otherwise to my descendants (my children and the descendants of my children) who survive me.

```
┌─────────────────────────────────────────────────┐
│                                                 │
└─────────────────────────────────────────────────┘
```

Choice Two: Nothing to my spouse; all to my descendants (my children and the descendants of my children) who survive me.

```
┌─────────────────────────────────────────────────┐
│                                                 │
└─────────────────────────────────────────────────┘
```

Choice Three: All to the following person if he or she survives me (insert the name of the person):

Choice Four: Equally among the following persons who survive me (insert the names of two or more persons):

---

6. Guardian of the Child's Person. If I have a child under age 18 and the child does not have a living parent at my death, I nominate the individual named below as First Choice as guardian of the person of such child (to raise the child). If the First Choice does not serve, then I nominate the Second Choice, and then the Third Choice, to serve. Only an individual (not a bank or trust company) may serve.

7. Special Provision of Property of Persons Under Age 25. (Optional—Unless you use this paragraph, assets that go to a child or other person who is under age 18 may be given to the parent of the person, or to the guardian named in paragraph 6 above as guardian of the person until age 18, and the court will require a bond; and assets that go to a child or other person who is age 18 or older will be given outright to the person. By using this paragraph you may provide that a custodian will hold the assets for the person until the person reaches any age between 18 and 25 which you choose.) If a beneficiary of this Will is between age 18 and 25, I nominate the individual or bank or trust company named below as First Choice as custodian of the property. If the First Choice does not serve, then I nominate the Second Choice, and then the Third Choice, to serve.

Insert any age between 18 and 25 as the age for the person to receive the property (if you do not choose an age, age 18 will apply):

I nominate the individual or bank or trust company named below as First Choice as executor. If the First Choice does not serve, then I nominate the Second Choice, and then the Third Choice, to serve.

Bond. My signature in this box means a bond is not required for any person named as executor. A bond may be required if I do not sign in this box:

No bond shall be required.

(Notice: You must sign this Will in the presence of two (2) adult witnesses. The witnesses must sign their names in your presence and in each other's presence. You must first read to them the following two sentences.)

This is my Will. I ask the persons who sign below to be my witnesses.

_____

Signature of Maker of Will

Signed on _____

at _____, California.

      (City)

(Notice to Witnesses: Two (2) adults must sign as witnesses. Each witness must read the following clause before signing. The witnesses should not receive assets under this Will.)

Each of us declares under penalty of perjury under the laws of the State of California that the following is true and correct:

a. On the date written below the maker of this Will declared to us that this instrument was the maker's Will and requested us to act as witnesses to it;

b. We understand this is the maker's Will;

c. The maker signed this Will in our presence, all of us being present at the same time;

d. We now, at the maker's request, and in the maker's and in each other's presence, sign below as witnesses;

e. We believe the maker is of sound mind and memory;

f. We believe that this Will was not procured by duress, menace, fraud, or undue influence;

g. The maker is age 18 or older; and

h. Each of us is now age 18 or older, is a competent witness, and resides at the address set forth after his or her name.

Dated:
Print Name Here:
Residence Address:
Dated:
Print Name Here:
Residence Address:

AT LEAST TWO WITNESSES MUST SIGN. NOTARIZATION ALONE IS NOT SUFFICIENT.

The following Sections of the law are included for reference.

DEFINITIONS AND RULES OF CONSTRUCTION

[Marginal numbers are the California Probate Code Sections.]

6200. Unless the provision or context clearly requires otherwise, these definitions and rules of construction govern the construction of this Chapter. [Statutory will.]

6201. "Testator" means a person choosing to adopt a California statutory will.

6202. "Spouse" means the testator's husband or wife at the time the testator signs a California statutory will.

6203. "Executor" means both the person so designated in a California statutory will and any other person acting at any time as the executor or administrator under a California statutory will.

6204. "Trustee" means both the person so designated in a California statutory will and any other person acting at any time as the trustee under a California statutory will.

6205. "Descendants" means children, grandchildren, and their lineal descendants of all generations with the relationship of parent and child at each generation being determined as provided in Section 6152. A reference to "descendants" in the plural includes a single descendant where the context so requires.

6206. A reference in a California statutory will to the "Uniform Gifts to Minors Act of any state" or the "Uniform Transfers to Minors Act of any state" includes both the Uniform Gifts to Minors Act of any state and Uniform Transfers to Minors Act of any state. A reference to a "custodian" means the person so designated in a California statutory will or any other person acting at any time as a custodian under a Uniform Gifts to Minors Act or Uniform Transfers to Minors Act.

6207. Masculine pronouns include the feminine, and plural and singular words include each other, where appropriate.

6208. (a) If a California statutory will states that a person shall perform an act, the person is required to perform that act.

(b) If a California statutory will states that a person may do an act, the person's decision to do or not to do the act shall be made in the exercise of the person's fiduciary powers.

6209. Whenever a distribution under a California statutory will is to be made to a person's descendants, the property shall be divided into as many equal shares as there are then living descendants of the nearest degree of living descendants and deceased descendants of that same degree who leave descendants then living, and each living descendant of the nearest degree shall receive one share and the share of each deceased descendant of that same degree shall be divided among his or her descendants in the same manner.

6210. "Person" includes individuals and institutions.

6211. Reference to a person "if living" or who "survives me" means a person who survives the decedent by 120 hours. A person who fails to survive the decedent by 120 hours is deemed to have predeceased the decedent for the purpose of a California statutory will, and the beneficiaries are determined accordingly. If it cannot be established by clear and convincing evidence that a person who would otherwise be a beneficiary has survived the decedent by 120 hours, it is deemed that the person failed to survive for the required period. The requirement of this Section that a person who survives the decedent must survive the decedent by 120 hours does not apply if the application of this 120-hour survival requirement would result in the escheat of property to the state.

CALIFORNIA PROBATE CODE SECTIONS APPLICABLE TO THE CALIFORNIA STATUTORY WILL

The following provisions of the California Probate Code are NOT a part of the California Statutory Will Form. [See Section 6223 below.] However, they relate to the California Statutory Will Form, and should be considered in making a decision to use or not use the California Statutory Will Form.

GENERAL PROVISIONS

(Marginal numbers are the California Probate Code Sections.)

6220. Any individual of sound mind and over the age of 18 may execute a California statutory will under the provisions of this chapter. [Chapter 6 of Part 1 of Division 6 of the Probate Code.]

6221. A California statutory will shall be executed only as follows:

The testator shall complete the appropriate blanks and shall sign the will.

Each witness shall observe the testator's signing and each witness shall sign his or her name in the presence of the testator.

6222. The execution of the attestation clause provided in the California statutory will by two or more witnesses satisfies Section 8220.

6223 (a) There is only one California statutory will.

(b) The California statutory will includes all of the following:

The contents of the California statutory will form set out in Section 6240, excluding the questions and answers at the beginning of the California statutory will.

By reference, the full texts of each of the following:

A. The definitions and rules of construction set forth in Article 1 (commencing with Section 6200).

B. The property disposition clauses adopted by the testator. If no property dispositions clause is adopted, Section 6224 shall apply.

C. The mandatory clauses set forth in Section 6241.

(c) Notwithstanding this section, any California statutory will or California statutory will with trust executed on a form allowed under prior law shall be governed by the law that applied prior to January 1, 1992.

6224. If more than one property disposition clause appearing in paragraphs 2 or 3 of a California statutory will is selected, no gift is made. If more than one property disposition clause in paragraph 5 of a California statutory will form is selected, or if none is selected, the residuary estate of a testator who signs a California statutory will shall be distributed to the testator's heirs as if the testator did not make a will.

6225. Only the texts of property disposition clauses and the mandatory clauses shall be considered in determining their meaning. Their titles shall be disregarded.

6226. (a) A California statutory will may be revoked and may be amended by codicil in the same manner as other wills.

(b) Any additions to or deletions from the California statutory will on the face of the California statutory will form, other than in accordance with the instructions, shall be given effect only where clear and convincing evidence shows that they would effectuate the clear intent of the testator. In the absence of such showing, the court either may determine that the addition or deletion is ineffective and shall be disregarded, or may determine that all or a portion of the California statutory will is invalid, whichever is more likely to be consistent with the intent of the testator.

(c) Notwithstanding Section 6110, a document executed on a California statutory will form is valid as a will if all of the following requirements are shown to be satisfied by clear and convincing evidence:

(1) The form is signed by the testator.

(2) The court is satisfied that the testator knew and approved of the contents of the will and intended it to have testamentary effect.

(3) The testamentary intent of the maker as reflected in the document is clear.

6227. (a) If after executing a California statutory will the testator's marriage is dissolved or annulled, the dissolution or annulment revokes any disposition of property made by the will to the former spouse and any nomination of the former spouse as executor, trustee, guardian, or custodian made by the will. If any disposition or nomination is revoked solely by this section, it is revived by the testator's remarriage to the former spouse.

(b) In case of revocation by dissolution or annulment:

(1) Property prevented from passing to a former spouse because of the revocation passes as if the former spouse failed to survive the testator.

(2) Provisions nominating the former spouse as executor, trustee, guardian, or custodian shall be interpreted as if the former spouse failed to survive testator.

(c) For purposes of this section, dissolution or annulment means any dissolution or annulment that would exclude the spouse as a surviving spouse within the meaning of Section 78. A decree of legal separation which does not terminate the status of husband and wife is not a dissolution or annulment for purposes of this section.

(d) This Section applies to any California statutory will, without regard to the time when the will was executed, but this Section does not apply to any case where the final judgment of dissolution or annulment of marriage occurs before January 1, 1985; and, if the final judgment of dissolution or annulment of marriage occurs before January 1, 1985, the case is governed by the law that applied prior to January 1, 1985.

6242. (a) Except as specifically provided in this chapter, a California statutory will shall include only the texts of the property disposition clauses and the mandatory clauses as they exist on the day the California statutory will is executed.

(b) Sections 6205, 6206, and 6227 apply to every California statutory will including those executed before January 1, 1985. Section 6211 applies only to California statutory wills executed after July 1, 1991.

(c) Notwithstanding Section 6222, and except as provided in subdivision (b), a California statutory will is governed by the law that applied prior to January 1, 1991, if the California statutory will is executed on a form that (1) was prepared for use under former Sections 56 to 56.14 inclusive, or former Sections 6200 to 6248, inclusive, of the Probate Code, and (2) satisfied the requirements of law that applied prior to January 1, 1992.

(d) A California statutory will does not fail to satisfy the requirements of subdivision (a) merely because the will is executed on a form that incorporates the mandatory clauses of Section 6241 that refer to former Section 1120.2. If the will incorporates the mandatory clauses with a reference to former Section 1120.2, the trustee has the powers listed in Article 2 (commencing with Section 16220 of Chapter 2 of Part 4 of Division 9).

6243. Except as specifically provided in this chapter, the general law of California applies to a California statutory will.

COMMENT: California Probate Code Section 6205 (quoted in the above Definitions and Rules of Construction) refers to California Probate Code Section 6152 which reads as follows:

Unless otherwise provided in the will:

(a) Except as provided in subdivision (b), halfbloods, adopted persons, persons born out of wedlock, stepchildren, foster children, and the issue of all such persons when appropriate to the class, are included in terms of class gift or relationship in accordance with the rules for determining relationship and inheritance rights for purposes of intestate succession.

(b) In construing a devise by a testator who is not the natural parent, a person born to the natural parent shall not be considered the child of that parent unless the person lived while a minor as a regular member of the household of the natural parent or of that parent's parent, brother, sister, spouse, or surviving spouse. In construing a devise by a testator who is not the adoptive parent, a person adopted by the adoptive parent shall not be considered the child of that parent unless the person lived while a minor (either before or after the adoption) as a regular member of the household of the adopting parent or of that parent's parent, brother, sister, or surviving spouse.

(c) Subdivisions (a) and (b) also apply in determining:

(1) Persons who would be kindred of the testator or kindred

of a surviving, deceased, or former spouse of the testator under Section 6147.

(2) Persons to be included as issue of a deceased devisee under Section 6147.

(3) Persons who would be the testator's or other designated person's heirs under Section 6151.

THE MANDATORY CLAUSES OF THIS CALIFORNIA STATUTORY WILL ARE AS FOLLOWS:

(a) **Intestate Disposition**. If the testator has not made an effective disposition of the residuary estate, the executor shall distribute it to the testator's heirs at law, their identities and respective shares to be determined according to the laws of the State of California in effect on the date of the testator's death relating to intestate succession of property not acquired from a predeceased spouse.

(b) **Powers of Executor**.

(1) In addition to any powers now or hereafter conferred upon executors by law, including all powers granted under the Independent Administration of Estate Act, the executor shall have the power to:

(A) Sell estate assets at public or private sale, for cash or on credit terms.

(B) Lease estate assets without restriction as to duration.

(C) Invest any surplus moneys of the estate in real or personal property, as the executor deems advisable.

(2) The executor may distribute estate assets otherwise distributable to a minor beneficiary to one of the following:

(A) The guardian of the minor's person or estate.

(B) Any adult person with whom the minor resides and who has the care, custody, or control of the minor.

(C) A custodian of the minor under the Uniform Transfer to Minors Act as designated in the California statutory will form.

The executor is free of liability and is discharged from any further accountability for distributing assets in compliance with the provisions of this paragraph.

(3) On any distribution of assets from the estate, the executor shall have the discretion to partition, allot, and distribute the assets in the following manner:

(A) In kind, including undivided interests in an asset or in any part of it.

(B) Partly in cash and partly in kind.

(C) Entirely in cash.

If a distribution is being made to more than one beneficiary, the executor shall have the discretion to distribute assets among them on a pro rata basis, with the assets valued as of the date of distribution.

(c) **Powers of Guardian**. A guardian of the person nominated in the California statutory will shall have the same authority with respect to the person of the ward as a parent having legal custody of a child would have. All powers granted to guardians in this paragraph may be exercised without court authorization.

LETTER TO SOCIAL SECURITY CERTIFYING DEATH

_____

(date)

_____

(Social Security Administration)

_____

(Street address or P.O. Box number)

_____

_____

(City)   *(State)*   *(Zip Code)*

To Whom It May Concern:

This is to inform you that_____,
(full name of the deceased)

whose Social Security number is _____, died on

_____.
(Month/day/year)

I am writing to you on behalf of_____
(Full name of survivor)

and would like to obtain an appointment as soon as possible to make an application for benefits. Please let me know where and when such a meeting can be arranged.

I will plan to bring the application documents with me to that meeting: a copy of the death certificate; a copy of the marriage certificate; copies of birth certificates of the deceased and survivors; the Social Security numbers of the survivors; and evidence of the deceased's recent earnings. If other information or documents are required, please let me know.

Sincerely yours,

_____

Signature

_____

(Typed or printed name)

_____

_____

(Street Address)

_____

(City, State, Zip Code)   *(Area code and telephone number)*

This is a copy of my mother's obituary, which my family wrote several days after she died. It was published in three local papers as well as the alumni magazines of Wellesley College and Cornell Medical School.

MODEL OBITUARY

FRANCES CAPRON KORB

Frances Capron Korb died on September 21, 2009, with the same unrelenting vigor and surety—for tomorrow will surely be another day full of sunlight and things to do and people to see—with which she lived her life at her beloved Friends House in Santa Rosa. She was 85 years old. Fran grew up in Montclair, New Jersey, and attended Wellesley College ('45) and Cornell Medical School ('49). She began her medical career as a pediatrician but focused on psychotherapy after her children were born. She studied with many of the great psychologists of our time, including Carl Rogers and James Bugental. She practiced in Saratoga, Palo Alto, and Santa Rosa, California.

In 1974, Fran joined several other therapists and social activists and established Thomas Creek Ranch—a communal environment in Forestville, California. While in Sonoma County, Fran continued her long tradition of training other therapists. While her many patients thrived because of her, her students revered her and they, as therapists, remain her most enduring legacy.

Fran adored her husband, Connell Korb, who passed away in 2003. Conn, among so many other things, helped Fran with her flower business in Bloomfield, sang in choirs throughout the Bay Area, and fixed toys for needy children in Sonoma County. Fran will be buried next to Conn and will join him, and the multitude of their friends, in eternity.

If you were family—and with Fran it was awfully hard not to be family—she made sure every day was filled with love and joy. In her youth, she loved to ride horses and she spent her summers on dude ranches in Wyoming. She was the delight of many a hardened cowboy who couldn't believe "the confidence and nerve of that Eastern girl." Her love of animals—particularly in her later years her cat, Harry Potter—was passed on to her children and grandchildren. Her keen desire to protect the planet and every living species was reflected in everything she did and prompted her to devote herself—after her first three careers—to education. She served as a docent for many years at the Bouverie Preserve and Audubon Canyon Ranch. For Sonoma County, she developed an interactive science program. With her snails and slugs and anything that felt good to the tender hands of an eighth-grade child she not only taught classes but also trained an army of volunteers to carry on the program. Her curriculum continues today.

Fran saw the world through the most tinted of glasses. Everyone was a friend and a peer. Everyone had something important to say or contribute. There was always another seat at the table. Miguel, the "guy who makes everything work at Friends House," said it best: "She had no curtains in her heart."

Fran contributed to every possible "good" cause in the world. Among her favorites were Heifer International, through which you can buy a goat for a family in Latin America; Doctors without Borders; the American Red Cross; the Grameen Foundation; and many, many more. If she were alive and writing this, Fran would say simply that you should give wherever and whenever your heart beckons. But she would never, ever say "in lieu of flowers" because she would urge you to plant some flowers, too; plant them everywhere. Donations may be made in her name to: Friends House Staff Year End Fund, 684 Benicia Drive, Santa Rosa, CA 95409.

She is survived by her four children, Terry, Scott, Kim, and Tory; her two stepchildren, Mitzi and John; and her four grandchildren, Jesse and Hoby Wedler and Lily and Carson Stokely. Her family wishes to extend its most heartfelt thanks to the staff and denizens of Friends House. She lived her last, many enriching years there in complete happiness. She died with the utmost dignity and with so many hands lifting her to heaven that the angels hardly had to flutter a wing to bring her home.

This form can be used to ask the county to transfer title of real estate.

Sample Affidavit of Surviving Spouse for
Change of Title to Real Estate

STATE OF _____

SS.

COUNTY OF _____

I, [wife's name], being first duly sworn on oath, depose and state as follows:

1. I am the surviving spouse of [husband's name], who died on the _____ day of ____, 2012.

2. The following described real estate was owned only by [husband's name] and this Affiant, as joint tenants with full rights of survivorship at the time of [husband's name]'s death:

[*legal description of property*]

3. I hereby request that the county clerk enter this information on the transfer books pursuant to section _____ of the [state] Code.

_____
[*wife's signature*]

Subscribed and sworn to before me this

_____day of _____, 20___.

_____

Notary Public in and for the State of_____

This form can be used to ask a brokerage firm or bank to transfer stocks or bonds.

SAMPLE AFFIDAVIT TO TRANSFER STOCK CERTIFICATES

[date]
[name & address of transfer agent]

Re: Securities of Scott Smith, deceased

Enclosed are stock certificates registered in the names of Scott Smith and Marsha Smith.

Certificate number: _____
Type of security: common stock
Number of shares [or for bonds, the face amount]: _____
Name of company: International Business Machines
These shares were owned as community property by Scott Smith and Marsha Smith. Please cancel the enclosed certificates and issue new certificates in the name of the surviving spouse, Marsha Smith, Social Security number ___-__-____.
I have enclosed a Stock Power, a certified copy of Mr. Smith's death certificate, and an Affidavit of Residence.
Sincerely,
Marsha Smith
[address]
[telephone]

This form can be used to demand that a life insurance company pay you the proceeds of a life insurance policy.

AFFIDAVIT FOR PAYMENT OF LIFE INSURANCE PROCEEDS

_____*(Date)*

_____
(Name of insurance company)

_____
(Street Address or P.O. Box No.)

_____
(City, State, Zip Code)

To Whom It May Concern:

_____ had a_____ policy
(Full name of deceased)   *(Type of policy)*

with your company. _____ was
                    (Full name of deceased)

Insured under policy number_____ and died_____.
Please send me whatever forms I should fill out if filing a claim for benefits on behalf of either the estate of
_____ or his/her survivors.
(Full name of deceased)

Sincerely yours,

_____

_____
(Signature)

_____
(Typed or printed name)

_____
(Street Address)

_____   _____
(City, State, Zip Code)   *(Area code and telephone number)*

211

Most states accept a will written completely by hand, signed, and dated as a valid will. It is called a "holographic will," and most states do not require witnesses. Here, we explain how to write a valid holographic will.

Instructions for Writing a Holographic Will

Many states accept handwritten—holographic—wills. These are wills written by the deceased in his or her own handwriting and signed. You usually do not need witnesses.

A legally binding holographic will requires that every word must be in the testator's own handwriting.

Properly dating a holographic will is essential to proving that the testator was of sound mind at the time the will was prepared. The date should appear at the top of the document and the form of the will should proceed as follows:

1. I, the testator, write this will with the intent of setting forth my wishes for the disposition of my estate after my death. As of the date of this will, I am of sound mind and am totally capable of determining my own affairs.

2. As to the money in my bank account, I want it to go to my . . . (son, daughter, wife, etc.)

3. As to my stocks and bonds (if any), I want them to go to my . . . (son, daughter, wife, etc.)

4. As to my furniture, television, car, and other personal property, etc. (if any), I want them to go to my . . . (son, daughter, wife, etc.)

5. As to my house, I want it to go to my . . . (son, daughter, wife, etc.)

The point in this particular form is to specifically set in order who will receive your personal property, real estate, and money after your death. In setting this in order, you must be specific.

The most important aspect of a holographic is its readability. The testator should carefully take time to ensure that the entire will is completely legible.

Remember, be specific as to your intents and wishes. The will may include your own personal statements as to why you prefer, for example, your son to receive your money instead of your wife.

Once you have written the will you should seal the will in an envelope, place tape over the seal, and send it to yourself by certified mail. When it is delivered, sign for it and staple the signed receipt to the envelope. Then place the will in a safe-deposit box, in a wall safe, or in a file cabinet for safekeeping. This process will ensure the integrity of the holographic will. Don't forget to sign the will.

Bibliography

Hall, Julie. *The Boomer's Burden: Dealing with Your Parents' Lifetime Accumulation of Stuff.* Nashville, TN: Thomas Nelson, 2007.

Jones, Karen. *Death for Beginners: Your No-Nonsense, Money-Saving Guide to Planning for the Inevitable.* Fresno, CA: Quill Driver Books, 2010.

Morgan, Ernest. *Dealing Creatively with Death: A Manual of Death Education and Simple Burial.* Hinesburg, VT: Upper Access Books, 2001.

Randolph, Mary. *The Executor's Guide: Settling a Loved One's Estate or Trust.* Berkeley, CA: Nolo Press, 2010.

Richter, Scott. *What to Do When Someone Dies: A Simple, Step-by-Step Guide for Family Members, Personal Representatives, and Executors.* Scott Richter, 2011.

Shaw, Eva. *What to Do When a Loved One Dies: A Practical and Compassionate Guide to Dealing with Death on Life's Terms.* Carlsbad, CA: Writeriffic Publishing, 2005.

Index

About the Authors

Scott Smith is the founder and CEO of Viant Capital LLC of San Francisco, a merchant bank specializing in technology investing. He was formerly a partner in Pillsbury Winthrop, a national law firm, where he specialized in corporate law and fiduciary duty.

Michael Castleman is the award-winning author of thirteen nonfiction books, four novels, and more than two thousand magazine and Web articles. His nonfiction deals with health and sexuality. His novels are mysteries set in San Francisco that deal, in part, with its history. Visit www.mcastleman.com.